Helping Special Student Groups

Lester Wilson, *Editor*

EW DIRECTIONS FOR COLLEGE LEARNING ASSISTANCE
URT V. LAURIDSEN, *Editor-in-Chief*

umber 7, March 1982

Paperback sourcebooks in
The Jossey-Bass Higher Education Series

Jossey-Bass Inc., Publishers
San Francisco • Washington • London

Helping Special Student Groups
Number 7, March 1982
    Lester Wilson, *Editor*

New Directions for College Learning Assistance Series
Kurt V. Lauridsen, *Editor-in-Chief*

New Directions for College Learning Assistance is published quarterly
by Jossey-Bass Inc., Publishers. Subscriptions, single-issue orders,
change of address notices, undelivered copies, and other
correspondence should be sent to *New Directions* Subscriptions,
Jossey-Bass Inc., Publishers, 433 California Street, San Francisco,
California 94104.

Editorial correspondence should be sent to the Editor-in-Chief,
Kurt V. Lauridsen, Director, Student Learning Center,
University of California, Berkeley, California 94720.

Library of Congress Catalogue Card Number LC 80-84261

International Standard Serial Number ISSN 0271-0617

International Standard Book Number ISBN 87589-879-3

Cover art by Willi Baum

Manufactured in the United States of America

Ordering Information

The paperback sourcebooks listed below are published quarterly and can be ordered either by subscription or as single copies.

Subscriptions cost $35.00 per year for institutions, agencies, and libraries. Individuals can subscribe at the special rate of $21.00 per year *if payment is by personal check.* (Note that the full rate of $35.00 applies if payment is by institutional check, even if the subscription is designated for an individual.) Standing orders are accepted.

Single copies are available at $7.95 when payment accompanies order, and *all single-copy orders under $25.00 must include payment.* (California, Washington, D.C., New Jersey, and New York residents please include appropriate sales tax.) For billed orders, cost per copy is $7.95 plus postage and handling. (Prices subject to change without notice.)

To ensure correct and prompt delivery, all orders must give either the *name of an individual* or an *official purchase order number.* Please submit your order as follows:

Subscriptions: specify series and subscription year.
Single Copies: specify sourcebook code and issue number (such as, CLA8).

Mail orders for United States and Possessions, Latin America, Canada, Japan, Australia, and New Zealand to:
Jossey-Bass Inc., Publishers
433 California Street
San Francisco, California 94104

Mail orders for all other parts of the world to:
Jossey-Bass Limited
28 Banner Street
London EC1Y 8QE

New Directions for College Learning Assistance Series
Kurt V. Lauridsen, *Editor-in-Chief*

Contents

Editor's Notes

A recurrent theme in this series of *New Directions for College Learning Assistance* sourcebooks is that the learning center of the 1980s will have to serve the entire college or university community. It has been pointed out in many sourcebook chapters that these centers have evolved from a more restricted base of operations, where they were centered in remediation and compensatory activities. Today, as increasing numbers of students with poor communications and quantitative skills enter college, learning center academic and counseling services will be in greater demand by a much larger segment of the undergraduate student population. Several contributing authors were also concerned with the problem of gaining faculty and administrative acceptance for this relatively new campus organization. With the arrival of ill-prepared students who no longer fit the customary social, racial and economic profiles, learning centers are more likely to win wider recognition for their programs, courses, and other supportive services.

The major philosophical idea behind the purpose and function of a learning center is that students should be able to learn independently, that their academic skills should be at a level to make this learning experience possible, and that the learning center can be of assistance in cases where learning problems make this experience unrealizable. The authors who have contributed chapters to this sourcebook would certainly endorse this idea. Most address the issue of how a learning center can provide help to selected student groups. Some also consider the perceptual problems that many students face in the new and unfamiliar university environment. Students who visit learning centers tend to feel that they are excluded from most academic and student-centered activities. Although their primary task is that of joining the ranks of the independent learner, they also need to see themselves as members of the college or university community. Getting them to the point of independence in learning and to a stage where they are actively engaged by the academic world around them—where they have entered the mainstream, in other words—is not easy. Learning centers can and should work in cooperation with other campus institutions towards this goal. Indeed, they cannot accomplish their work unaided.

How learning center assistance is delivered to individual students and to student groups with special needs depends on administrative decisions made at the individual college or university. In this volume, certain groups have been singled out for purposes of illustration—underprepared students, students with physical handicaps, students with learning disabilities, and students for whom English is a second language. As the authors discuss different approaches to working with these special groups, the reader will perhaps find useful information that can be applied to his particular campus situation. It will be noted that they have also attempted to place their student groups in the wider context of general learning center services and the academic community as a whole.

Two chapters in this volume propose a more inclusive approach to the question of how to get students to a level where they can take over for themselves. Coleman, in the first chapter, discusses some of the stumbling blocks that students, faculty, and administrators face in striving to achieve this goal. Into her treatment of specific problem areas, she weaves analyses of the kinds of academic and counseling supportive services that learning centers should have and how centers can be integrated into general college or university efforts to mainstream special student groups. Nieves, in a later chapter, raises the question of how to give students self-management skills that will help them to achieve the desired independence in learning.

Two points about terminology are appropriate here. Many terms have been used to describe college students with poor academic skills. The term *underprepared* will be used in this sourcebook, mainly because it seems most descriptive of the students under discussion. Likewise, in dealing with the topics of compensatory courses and academic support services, the term *developmental* will be used in preference to the term *remedial*. The former is both more inclusive and less judgmental.

The reader will find several descriptions of actual learning centers in the eight chapters of this volume. The authors have no illusion that the operations of one center will be applicable in their entirety to the situation on any other campus. However, they have all had many years of experience in the field, and undoubtedly some of their ideas will be of practical use. Also, since these centers can be thought of as model, an understanding of their activities should have value for administrators and other interested university groups who are not directly involved in learning center activities.

Lester Wilson
Editor

Lester Wilson is director of Special Academic Services at the Brooklyn Center of Long Island University. He has directed the LIU/Brooklyn Learning Center for the past five years.

*The reconciliation of access and excellence in the face
of student diversity, declining enrollments, and scarce
resources will be a major challenge to education
during the 1980s.*

Reconciling Access with Excellence: The Challenge of Educating Underprepared Students

Joan E. Coleman

The reconciliation of access and excellence in the face of student diversity
and scarce resources poses a major challenge to education during the
present decade. As colleges and universities continue to provide opportunity and quality education to a student population with a wide range of
abilities, learning needs, and backgrounds, they will find it necessary to
address fundamental issues relating to the learning requirements of students and to the extent to which these needs can be generalized to the
larger student body. The educational experiences that underprepared students have had prior to the freshman year rarely leave them with all
the academic, intellectual, and personal skills that they need in order to
compete successfully in college. Historically, special programs for these
students have sought to remedy deficiencies and to compensate for socioeconomic disadvantages. More recently, educators have come to recognize
that these approaches are fragmented and address only isolated needs.
Most educators would now agree that it is necessary to deal both with the
total student and with the learning environment in which he functions.

L. Wilson (Ed.). *New Directions for College Learning Assistance:
Helping Special Student Groups*, no. 7. San Francisco: Jossey-Bass, March 1982.

Underprepared students have always had widely divergent abilities, motivations, and perceptions about college. However, there are now many new special groups of students on campus, and in their ranks are substantial numbers of students who normally would be termed *underprepared*. Also, increasing numbers of regularly admitted college students exhibit communication skills deficiencies once thought to be characteristic of special program students. The learning needs of these various student groups represent a dilemma for learning centers and special academic support programs, which have been among the few campus institutions available to help them. As colleges and universities explore ways in which to assist these heretofore underserved students, they should recognize the need to shift operationally from the selection of potential to the development of potential. In this chapter, some problem areas involved in this process will be defined, and the role that learning centers can play in ensuring that students are provided with the kind of instruction and the type of environment that gives them a chance for academic success will be reassessed.

Freshman Assessment

Assessment procedures are based on the recognition that a certain amount of learning is prerequisite for learning other tasks. In addition to a cognitive history, an underprepared student brings to the classroom an affective history and a complex set of interests, attitudes, and academic and personal self-images. Some of these views are related to and reinforced by life experience, while others are specifically related to the school learning environment. Benjamin Bloom (1976) has discussed student affect as a major factor in learning. His findings show a significant relationship between affective characteristics and measures of school achievement. Bloom estimates that "affective entry characteristics"—a student's affective history—accounts for up to one fourth of the variation in measures of academic performance. His evidence, which is supported by the experience of special program staff, suggests that entry characteristics, such as motivation, attitudes and expectations towards learning, self-image, and the ability to persist in the face of frustration, can be altered. Bloom's research shows that it is possible to maximize achievement by improving affective as well as cognitive characteristics.

Historically, learning assistance programs have recognized the importance of affective factors in the learning process and provided various workshops and skills courses that address affective learning. However, the decreasing levels of preparedness of various student groups suggest that a more structured approach to this problem is needed.

Exploration and development of assessment tools that measure and diagnose attitudinal strengths and weaknesses and that prescribe corrective measures hold out promise for enhancing students' ability to persist. Presently, many colleges use basic skills or placement examinations to measure academic skills and prescribe appropriate course placement. A similar procedure should be developed for the affective skills area. An additional task, that of exploring the interaction between affective and cognitive learning, calls for collaboration between the office of research and members of the learning center staff. For example, some of the most recent research in remediation indicates that the underprepared student's failure or success is frequently determined by affective variables (Piesco, 1978). Because learning center staff—instructors, counselors, tutors—are involved constantly in assessment and alteration of affective characteristics, they can provide the necessary perceptions, behavioral observations, and alternative frames of reference that those who are actively engaged in the research will need. Accordingly, research staff can supply technical assistance and suggest ways of interpreting patterns of student behavior. The research component can also provide guidance in the analysis of perceptions and in understanding causal relationships. If this interchange is coordinated, it can lead to useful data and conclusive research on the interaction of affective and cognitive characteristics in learning.

On the question of assessment of entering freshmen, it should be noted that learning centers, as a rule, do not conduct collegewide evaluations of student population groups, including freshmen. At some institutions, Educational Opportunity Programs (EOP) conduct the only systematic assessment of student entry skills. In other cases, the admissions office or a systemwide testing office has this responsibility. Learning centers, however, receive a continuous flow of students, who, because of placement scores or other referrals, require their services. Clearly, planning and service delivery would be facilitated if centers were directly involved in freshman assessment procedures and in determination of the kinds of services needed.

As participants in the assessment process, learning center staff would find it useful to receive computer printouts of test scores and placement results on a regular basis so that they could identify as early as possible both the students who need intervention and the kinds of intervention needed. Some underprepared students will require a comprehensive program of basic skills and developmental instruction. Others will need only tutoring or counseling. It should be noted that all disadvantaged students will not need remediation. For example, high-achieving, low-income minority students may require intensive counseling and intellectual orientation if they are to learn an institution's latent curriculum and integrate its goals and expectations with their own. Recent data (Treisman, 1981) from the Professional Development Program, University of California, Berkeley, challenge the notion of the automatic survival of talented minority students. These data also indicate that persistence and academic achievement are inversely correlated with good academic performance in high school among low-income minority students, especially males. This points to a particular vulnerability to the traditional college environment and its demands and to the psychological effect of poor performance on students who have developed an image of high achievement. Reports from this program also suggest that there may be factors in the institutional environment that operate more severely on talented minority students than on others.

Another area in which special attention to assessment will be needed is mathematics. Many underprepared students enter college with serious affective and cognitive deficiencies in mathematics. These characteristics call for special assessment of their learning needs in this area. Recent data from a National Assessment of Educational Progress Study (1979) document a general decline in mathematics scores among high school graduates. This decline, together with a projection (Carnegie Council, 1980) that the number of high school graduates in 1986 will be 15 percent less than in 1975, threatens a major shortfall in the number of graduates with a strong mathematics background. The problem is compounded by the quality of secondary school mathematics instruction, outdated mathematics curricula, and limited course offerings, particularly in some low-income high schools, where basic mathematics is the only course in this subject that is required for graduation. Proficiency in higher mathematics is essential to the study of science and to success in any science-related career. Underprepared students, by virtue of their early negative feelings toward mathematics and their limited course experience in mathematics, often are seriously underrepresented in mathematics, science, and engineering programs. Learning centers can play a special role in providing outreach for early identification and career workshops for early orientation of students in this group who are interested in mathematics or the sciences but who require intensive skills building and supplementary instruction in order to pursue a major in these fields.

Intellectual Orientation to College

One of the reasons why some colleges fail to define the learning needs of their new student populations adequately is that they lack a clear definition of the purposes and uses of undergraduate education for students in general. Their lack of objectives is reflected in the following comment from a 1968 Stanford University curriculum committee report: "The objective toward which curriculum planning should strive is, to the extent possible, to let the teacher teach what he wants to teach and the student learn what he wants to learn" (Stanford University, 1968, p. 12). Generally, colleges and universities do not attempt in any systematic way to guide the educational and personal goals that their students could want or expect to achieve as a result of their four or five years of study; nor do they assist students in learning or negotiating the hidden curriculum of the institution—the invisible but implied set of attitudes, judgments, rules, values, priorities, and assigned roles that underlies faculty and administrative perceptions and assessments (Overly, 1970). Students are left on their own to integrate and make sense of facts, theories, principles, systems, and concepts encountered in the many courses that they undertake. Bok (1974) points out that students today are a highly diverse group with widely varying interests and aspirations. They lack the experience to undertake the responsibility of making course and career choices unaided. He suggests that students could profit more from a knowledge of what instructors hope to accomplish in their courses than from a brief description of the subject matter to be covered. Bok recommends instruction that provides an opportunity for students to think about their entire undergraduate experience comprehensively and to ponder a variety of views from various educators concerning the purpose toward which the four years could be directed.

Special program and other students who lack the traditional preparation for college need assistance in developing an intellectual orientation toward college. Usually unfamiliar with the broad philosophical purposes of college and with its inherent values and expectations, they often perceive their new educational environment as an extension of high school. Many underprepared students have made sudden decisions to come to college. Often, they have been prompted to do so by others or simply by the availability of special program funds. Once there, they encounter a psychologically, culturally, and intellectually overwhelming experience. Without the benefit of a historical or humanistic context, they are unable to evaluate, utilize, and manipulate this experience effectively. Their predicament is expressed aptly in such questions as "Why study writing? Or mathematics, or poetry, or art?" "What does liberal arts mean?" "Why do I have to take this course if I am not interested in it and if it won't help me to become a nurse, or an engineer, or an elementary school teacher?" If a student lacks a historical or personal perspective of the various courses and academic disciplines of the college, he will be inclined to a rote, fragmented, and isolated approach to learning. To the extent that he is unable to integrate the many facets of his academic experience, his motivation and sense of purpose will not be at an optimum.

In recent years, educators have stressed the importance of college orientation and career counseling programs in helping students to adjust to college and make meaningful academic and career decisions. One important part of the orientation process introduces students to the relationship between education and the traditional goals and purposes of American society. Students must understand that an institution's educational goals are only a reflection of larger societal goals and that colleges and universities help to develop ways of thinking, systems of value, traditional beliefs, and practices that are considered essential for successful participation in society. In view of this responsibility, it is incumbent upon colleges and universities to attempt to get students to visualize their education as occurring within a general societal, social, and intellectual context that includes the student, the college, the family, and the community.

Underprepared students bring fully developed, coherent, cultural assumptions with them. Students must learn not only new ways of viewing the world, but they must also revise at least some of their older assumptions. This process of re-education, though painful and uncertain, can be facilitated if colleges undertake the responsibility in a structured, supportive, and enlightened manner. In a report on Kean College, Bruffee (1979) points to the need for faculty, administrators, and students to overcome the myth of "college material": the traditional assumption that, to succeed in college, students must arrive on campus with a uniform cultural and educational background. He views the process of acquiring a college education as one involving both the acquisition of knowledge and a larger and deeper sort of change affecting the total individual.

Some colleges and universities now sponsor courses that are designed to deal with this process of re-education. A course on the dynamics of university adjustment is offered at the University of California, Los Angeles, and Kean College in Union, New Jersey, titles a course Values, Choices, and Careers. Typically, these courses are meant to orient special program students or others to college and the liberal arts and sciences curriculum and introduce them to education as a process of socialization as well as of learning. By virtue of their structure and the expertise of their staff, learning centers are in a unique position to offer orientation courses and workshops to all entering students. In these sessions, students can be prepared to confront the values, views, and assumptions that they will encounter, and they can be helped to understand that these are not truths but rather the manner in which a group or a culture look at society and the world. Course instructors present and explore various philosophies of education, with the goal of teaching students to develop the practice of pursuing meaning and value personally and purposefully in order to make sense of and bring order to their lives. A seminar or workshop format for such courses provides a context in which students can pose their questions, integrate their learning, and synthesize basic skills as readily as they are required.

Basic Competence Standards

An area of serious academic concern in which learning centers can make effective contributions relates to the long-term decline in student basic skills levels. Underprepared students have always required basic skills instruction, but, as already noted here, many new student groups now on campus have similar skills deficiencies. In addition to basic skills courses and supportive services, minimum competency testing is often used to remedy this situation. One of the results of the back-to-basics movement of the late sixties and early seventies was that classroom instruction was often geared to proficiency tests. In many instances, these tests emphasized the most superficial aspects of learning in the content areas, since they focused on the recall of facts and information, not on the understanding of conceptual schemes. Such a narrow perspective tends to minimize learning by holding students to a norm and by lowering teacher expectations of student achievement. Since application and conceptual understanding are not stressed, students cannot build on what they learn.

There is some evidence that proficiency test results do not provide an adequate measure of achievement. In a cross-cultural study, Brooks (1975) found that some students use memory rather than analysis in problem solving. As a result, students can show achievement gains on basic skills tests, while in fact they are falling behind in areas requiring complex cognitive processes. Many underprepared students complete developmental courses in mathematics, reading comprehension, and writing with some degree of success, yet they fail to pass introductory courses in various disciplines. Analysis of student failure in these courses suggests a need for a kind of transitional instruction to bridge the gap between the learning of isolated skills and successful application of these skills in more advanced courses (Coleman and Jemmott, 1976). These findings also reinforce the desirability of expanding the definition of competence and in reassessing the instruction designed to achieve it.

An approach that seeks only to remedy basic skills is fragmented and ignores other cognitive and affective skills that are necessary for academic success. To address this problem, some learning centers and special programs have developed courses in which basic principles and terminology are selected from introductory courses. The purpose of these transitional or developmental offerings is to help students comprehend the concept of an academic discipline, to analyze and synthesize some of the inherent thought patterns and structures of various disciplines, and to become more familiar with related college texts. These courses can be credit-bearing, since they combine basic skills instruction with college-level content. They do not duplicate regular introductory college courses, since they emphasize general social science, literature, or science skills and do not impart specialized content, unless it is necessary for the student to acquire the skills in question.

Courses of this nature are offered at Rutgers University in the Academic Foundations Department, at University of Wisconsin, Parkside, in the Collegiate Skills Program, and at Brooklyn College-City University of New York in the Department of Educational Services. They provide a bridge to freshmen and sophomore liberal arts courses and involve students in the intellectual thought of the college, thereby increasing student motivation.

All too often, developmental programs that operate in isolation from college or university faculty adopt minimal expectations for student performance. The concept of functional literacy, which relates competence to the academic and institutional milieu in which students must function (Cohen, 1979), requires teaching faculty to be involved in establishing exit criteria and in identifying the elusive skills for which blanket cutoff scores do not account. This issue is timely for learning center personnel, since they have both experience and expertise in the skills-building process. A joint learning center-faculty task force is an excellent mechanism for achieving collaboration in areas of academic, intellectual, and personal skills identification for students at a given institution. This approach has been used successfully at Brooklyn College, where a group of special program and academic departmental faculty developed a comprehensive preparatory curriculum combining skills and content material. The proposals that emerged from this group were brought before a faculty council. The point at issue here is that teams composed of faculty and learning center personnel can be very effective in devising a course of study that goes beyond a strict emphasis on the basics to provide comprehensive instruction for underprepared students.

Faculty-Student Interaction

Historically, learning centers have sought to address student-related characteristics, such as counseling, orientation, and career assistance, that are related to the persistence of underprepared students. While learning center staff cannot alter institution-related variables singlehand-edly, they can use their knowledge and experience to provide impetus and direction for institutions in modifying or changing existing characteristics that contribute to attrition and that reinforce characteristics that enhance persistence. A significant finding of Ramist (1981, p. 2) is that student-faculty interaction is a major factor in the retention of underprepared and other student groups. As he states, "Interaction between faculty and students leads to academic and social integration in the college and is related to higher grades, greater self-perceived intellectual growth, and self-esteem. One study (Astin, 1977) reports in fact that it has the strongest relationship to student satisfaction with college." In spite of this and similar findings, few institutions have in place systems or structures for creating incentives and rewards to encourage contact between faculty and students. There are a number of approaches that learning centers can use to encourage faculty-student interaction both formally and informally. First, learning centers can provide supplementary or alternative learning situations that expand the actual time that students spend in active learning. Such strategies can utilize both departmental and learning center faculty. Second, learning center staff can work with their institutions to design programs and services that place faculty in regular contact with students, especially with entering freshman. Learning centers can be most effective in both roles if they attempt to coordinate and integrate their activities with those of the traditional departments.

Administrative Issues

Much has already been said on learning centers in this chapter, but it has been within the framework of the academic community in general. Because of their particular association with underprepared students and with opportunity programs, an examination of some problem areas related to administration, service delivery systems, and funding support seems appropriate at this point.

Organizational Structure. The place of the learning center in an institution's organizational structure is generally indicative of the institution's attitudes toward the learning needs of its underprepared student population. Initially, in the late sixties and early seventies, learning centers and similar academic support programs operated as separate, autonomous entities, often with informal lines of authority. As the function of these centers expanded, they were placed under the administrative, academic, or student service areas of the college. Sometimes, centers reported to the financial aid, business, or minority affairs offices and consequently were subject to the funding and other priorities of these units. Additionally, this placement limited both the learning center's actual role and activities and student and faculty perceptions of that role. Particular problems occurred in cases where centers had been placed under minority affairs or affirmative action offices or where a center director had joint responsibility for these offices. Directors could be called upon to work with a department chairman on curriculum development one day and to charge him with discrimination in hiring practices on the next. Such arrangements involve a conflict of interest and are untenable. Further, they are unjustified, since learning centers do not serve minority populations exclusively (more than 50 percent of the nontraditional student population on college campuses today is white). Learning centers, clearly, should be placed under the academic arm of the college, where their instructional role can be supported and integrated with the general academic program offerings.

Duplication of Efforts. A number of federal, state, and local programs designed to serve special groups—disadvantaged, talented, physically disabled, learning-disabled, low-income—can be found in a single institution. In some cases, these programs supplement one another's efforts; in others, they result in duplication or fragmented services. For example, a special services project student who is supported by federal funds can appear on the eligibility rolls of the campus EOP program and at the same time may be receiving support services at the learning center. This confusing situation raises questions of fiscal accountability, and it can impede effective service delivery and academic monitoring of students. Also, when students with similar academic profiles are serviced by different programs, one group can be afforded services that are unavailable to the other. Considerable duplication, fragmentation, and fiscal inefficiency can be eliminated if one of these programs serves as the administrative umbrella for the others. Such a structure allows for maximum use of the available resources and promotes uniform delivery of services.

Funding. Historically, institutional funding for academic support services to underprepared students has been connected to educational opportunity programs, and many learning centers have been spawned by these programs. While EOP programs for disadvantaged students have a general philosophical commitment to serving underprepared students, their guidelines, in fact, restrict the use of program funds to support of EOP students. The original intent of special program legislation cannot therefore be violated, and the original mission of providing educational opportunity for economically and educationally disadvantaged students must be maintained. It is obvious, therefore, that if learning center services are to be expanded to meet the needs of underprepared students in general, additional institutional or outside support is required.

Operating budgets for learning centers come from a combination of federal, state, and local grants, foundation support, and institutional allocations. Many colleges and universities support their centers through registration and tuition fees. Others utilize special program funds while providing some supplementary assistance. If learning centers are to expand their services during the present decade, they will probably find it difficult, if not impossible, to increase funding from public sources significantly. Private foundation support will be awarded only on a very competitive basis. In a very real sense, centers are going to have to turn to their local institution and seek additional funds through a reallocation of existing funds, resources, and faculty. Some colleges, for example, allow sections of freshman literature to run with less than a dozen students in each, while learning center instructors are required to teach basic skills classes to thirty or forty students at a time. A reallocation of funds and a revision of institutional priorities is clearly called for in cases like these. If underprepared students are not afforded the best instruction possible, they will fail to persist into the junior and senior years. This attrition, in turn, will decrease prospective upper division enrollment. Thus, faculty members have a vested interest in maintaining and perhaps even in increasing funding support for learning centers.

Delivery of Services. Instructors and counselors have observed that students who need academic support services the most do not actively seek them (Roueche, 1973). Therefore, the referral or walk-in policy for learning centers probably will not reach these students in a timely and effective way. Even when skills assistance is prescribed by an instructor, this usually happens sometime during the semester, after the student has demonstrated difficulty in coping with course material. Experience with underprepared students suggests that early identification of needs, at the entry level if possible, and mandatory, systematic provision of skills assistance can be both preventive and corrective. To this purpose, some centers have collaborated with other campus agencies to identify problem freshman courses and to offer workshops based on course content. Students are required to register for these workshops when they register for the courses in question, so they are much more inclined to take the workshops seriously. Establishing procedures to make sure that all students who need academic support services and instruction do indeed receive this assistance should be a major concern of learning center administrators. Opportunity programs for disadvantaged students have always had program guidelines that held institutions accountable for the provision of defined services to the target groups. On many campuses, no such guidelines exist for the general underprepared student population, nor is there any mandated requirement for institutional accountability. A more uniform system for testing, placement, instruction, and monitoring is needed, and learning centers are ideally situated to undertake this responsibility.

Department Status for Learning Centers. Learning center directors usually find the separate, autonomous unit model attractive. Unfortunately, this model tends to be most expendable in times of fiscal stringency. Recognizing this vulnerability, some directors have explored other organizational models that are more in line with the traditional structures in operation at their institution. Administrators who would like for their centers to take on a more traditional academic role might consider working with their institution to develop a department or divisional model. Such units are now in operation at both four-year and community colleges throughout the country. They are known, for example, as *academic foundations, educational services,* or *developmental education* and have as their focus a comprehensive, interdisciplinary, and developmental curriculum.

To illustrate this organizational model, let us imagine an interdisciplinary department of developmental learning organized with the full status, responsibilities, and authority of an academic department, including the power to appoint, promote, and tenure faculty, to develop curriculum, and to offer credit-bearing courses. This kind of department would focus on a comprehensive prefreshman summer and freshman-year curriculum for all entering underprepared students, supplemented by other skills courses and workshops as required by the general student population. This structural arrangement would house professional faculty in skills areas, and other faculty members would be assigned to teach transitional courses. A professional counseling staff and a tutorial component would be based in the department as well. This type of organization would benefit from faculty members who were committed to developmental learning in their own discipline areas, and it would allow for cooperative attempts to develop teaching strategies, methodologies, and course materials for use in improving student performance. Generally, institutions limit the number of credits toward graduation that students can accumulate in such a department.

To illustrate this concept again, let us imagine a developmental learning center that coordinates the services for all underprepared students. However, it is not a recognized academic department. Unlike the unit described in the preceding paragraph, it must draw on faculty of other departments to provide course instruction. The drawback here is that the center director has no real authority over the choice of faculty members who teach courses in the center or who offer developmental courses under the umbrella of other departments.

Both models should utilize existing learning center and special program staff as well as interested faculty who are, or who can be made, sensitive to the learning needs of underprepared students. Nothing precludes selection of traditionally trained faculty members. In fact, possibilities for successful collaboration and joint planning with departments and university administrators are enhanced by the aura of credibility that such instructors bring to the center. All staff and faculty members, in addition to being proficient in their respective disciplines, should know the concepts and methodologies basic to developmental education. They also need to be familiar with individualized instruction and other techniques that are effective in working with underprepared students.

The special knowledge and skills of learning center staff members often are lost due to the isolation of the center and its activities from the academic interchange and operation of the college. The departmental model creates an opportunity for learning center staff to share and interact with traditional faculty around issues and problems in learning that relate to students in general. Joint departmental seminars and workshops serve to present and disseminate information on successful instructional techniques and interventions. Another advantage of the departmental model is that it allows for faculty-staff rotation programs in which departmental faculty are invited to spend a semester or some other unit of time on assignment to the learning center and vice versa. Learning center faculty may want to teach a regular college course in their area of specialty or do team teaching in traditional academic departments. Summer workshops and training programs provide a means for orienting and training faculty to take on these new assignments.

In general, discussions and negotiations required for establishment of the departmental model suggested here are often characterized by budgetary, political, and territorial considerations, to the detriment of educational and pedagogical merits. However, it is possible to arrive at mutually acceptable arrangements in which the concerns of students, faculty, and learning center staff are addressed. In the long run, learning center directors will discover that more can be gained from active cooperation with departments and individual faculty members than from attempts to remain autonomous and keep their centers at a distance from the activities of their faculty and administration colleagues.

Conclusion

The preceding discussion of the learning needs of underprepared students describes a number of roles and models for learning centers and learning assistance programs. These centers have a dual role with their student populations and within the college or university setting. Underprepared students and other special student groups experience a significant gap between college course offerings and their previous educational experience. It is the challenge of the learning center to bridge this gap by enhancing the development of student skills and personal growth on the one hand and by encouraging curricular and institutional changes in areas that affect these students on the other. Expansion of existing learning center models and strategies provides an ideal means of addressing the diverse learning needs of the entire student population, including the underprepared student group. The expanded models, which utilize existing resources and learning center staff expertise, could maximize student academic and personal development. To the extent that these models can be established successfully, institutional attitudes and policies will be modified in favor of continued support for these centers and their activities.

It is obvious that the 1980s will see a reassessment of many areas of direct concern to learning center directors and staff members. Clearly, available resources will be the focus of attention and discussion for some years to come. Colleges and universities, in the final analysis, will have to reconcile the seemingly divergent goals: access and excellence. However, these goals are interdependent, for, to the degree that an institution enhances learning for all student groups, it moves towards excellence.

References

Astin, A. *Four Critical Years: Effects of College on Beliefs, Attitudes, and Knowledge.* San Francisco: Jossey-Bass, 1977.

Bloom, B. *Human Characteristics and School Learning.* New York: McGraw-Hill, 1976.

Bok, D. "On the Purposes of Undergraduate Education." *Daedalus,* 1974, *103* (4), 159-174.

Brooks, I. "A Cross-Cultural Study of Concept Learning." Unpublished doctoral dissertation, University of Calgary, 1975.

Bruffee, K. "The Kean College Developmental Studies Program: Evaluation and Suggestions for the Future." Unpublished report, Kean College, 1979.

Carnegie Council on Policy Studies in Higher Education. *Three Thousand Futures: The Next Twenty Years in Higher Education.* San Francisco: Jossey-Bass, 1980.

Coleman, J., and Jemmott, R. "Position Paper." New York: Department of Educational Services, Brooklyn College, City University of New York, 1976.

National Assessment of Educational Progress. *Changes in Mathematical Achievement.* Denver: National Assessment of Educational Progress, 1979.

Overly, N. (Ed.). *The Unstudied Curriculum.* Washington, D.C.: Association for Supervision and Curriculum Development, National Education Association, 1970.

Piesco, J. *A Review of Research on Remedial Programs at the City University of New York.* New York: City University of New York, 1978.

Ramist, L. "College Student Attrition and Retention." *Findings.* Educational Testing Service, 1981, *6* (2), 1-4.

Roueche, J., and Kirk, R. *Catching Up*. San Francisco: Jossey-Bass, 1973.
Stanford University. "The Study of Education at Stanford." *Curriculum Report,* 1968, *2* (1), 12.
Treisman, U. *The Mathematics Science Workshop: A Progress Report*. Berkeley, Calif.: Professional Development Program, University of California, 1981.

Joan E. Coleman is a consultant to the Ford Foundation and the Office of Special Programs, City University of New York. As a member of the faculty at Brooklyn College, she designed and implemented academic support and developmental education programs.

*Underprepared students' academic skills levels vary
from campus to campus, depending on entrance
requirements and academic standards. However, all
these students face the difficult task of entering the
mainstream of their college community.*

Learning Center Services
for Underprepared Students

William Collins
Lester Wilson

The term *nontraditional* is used in academic circles to describe college
and university undergraduates who are dissimilar to the generations of
students who applied for and were accepted for full matriculation in the
past. It has been applied to the academically underprepared, minority
students, students for whom English is a second language, older students,
and students who have distinctive physical or learning disabilities. During the 1970s, in particular, it was a code word for the radically different
and a popular euphemism for disadvantaged minority students. As the
decade progressed, colleges and universities recruited more and more of
these nontraditional students, partly out of genuine interest and concern,
partly in response to social and political pressures, partly to offset a continuing decline in undergraduate enrollment. Today, there are so many
nontraditional students on campus that the term has lost much of its
original meaning.

   Amid the variety of students to whom this term has been applied,
academically underprepared students have always received the most attention and notoriety. Many, though certainly not all, have racial or ethnic
minority backgrounds. They are from inner-city high schools, and have

L. Wilson (Ed.). *New Directions for College Learning Assistance:
Helping Special Student Groups*, no. 7. San Francisco: Jossey-Bass, March 1982.

grown up in blighted and racially segregated neighborhoods. Their poor high school preparation and academic skills normally would have left them unqualified for college-level work. However, federal and state legislation of the 1960s and 1970s, itself a reflection of changing societal attitudes, provided funding for a wide range of compensatory programs and services. Open admissions, new recruitment policies, and special admit programs were introduced. These have been largely responsible for making colleges and universities accessible to such students.

Access, however, implies far more than a decision to admit underprepared students. Their deficient academic backgrounds made it difficult, and sometimes impossible, for them to cope with the academic and personal demands that were placed on them. During the first great influx of these students in the late 1960s and early 1970s, postsecondary institutions hastily devised developmental programs that were supposed to bring the members of this group up to the preparation levels of regularly admitted students. Years of inadequate training were to be corrected within two or three semesters. Not unexpectedly, these efforts were not uniformly successful. Often, they foundered, either because they were poorly conceived in the first place or because students were bewildered and frustrated. Since they were being asked to do so much in such a short time, it is not difficult to understand why so many reacted with suspicion and hostility.

The crisis atmosphere that accompanied the advent of these underprepared students to college campuses has subsided, due partially to a general decline in student militancy and a return to an atmosphere reminiscent of the 1950s, partially to steps taken by the academic community itself. In any case, the scope of the problem is much more clearly perceived in 1982 than it was in 1972. Although comprehensive solutions have yet to be found, it is still true that colleges and universities have now developed considerable expertise in ways of helping the underprepared student. Specially funded programs, development courses, tutoring, academic and personal counseling services—all now contribute to integration of these students into the mainstream of college life. Gradually, with the proliferation of support services and programs, there emerged a new campus institution that incorporated the diverse and sometimes diffuse compensatory efforts into a rationalized, administratively sound organization. Referred to on many campuses as the learning center, this new component has come to bear a good deal of the responsibility for enabling underprepared students to succeed as college undergraduates.

Learning centers are now as much a part of campus life as the underprepared students whom they serve. Interest in their operations and effect on underprepared student retention is widespread. Five years ago,

Sullivan (1977) listed and categorized the student services of more than 1,400 learning centers; more have appeared since then. Literature on this subject includes surveys of learning center structures (Cross, 1971, 1976) and descriptions of the various design options (Karwin, 1973; Maxwell, 1978; Peterson, 1975). Enright and Kerstiens (1980) reviewed the evolution of learning centers for the second *New Developments for College Learning Assistance* sourcebook. Professional organizations, local and national conferences, institutes, and workshops add to this atmosphere of intense pedagogical effort. A small but potentially significant movement is under way to advance opportunities for graduate training and degrees to learning center personnel. All these encouraging developments undoubtedly will enhance the academic credibility of the learning center as a viable campus institution and be reflected in more effective ways of assisting the underprepared student population.

The learning center response to these students will vary from one college or university to another. The variations will stem both from institutional goals, academic policies, and requirements and from students' levels of academic skills preparation. Thus, no one operational mode is universally applicable. The different approaches of two institutions have been selected for purposes of illustration in this chapter: the Learning Skills Center at Cornell University and its counterpart at the Brooklyn Center of Long Island University. In both examples, it will be noted that the centers have adapted services, methodologies, and materials to the needs of their undergraduate student population and adapted both to the context and academic confines of the standards and admissions policies of their institutions.

Learning Centers in Two Different Settings

Cornell University. Cornell University, founded in 1865 by Ezra Cornell, is a private, nonsectarian university. It is also the land-grant institution of New York state and a member of the Ivy League. As such, the student body is highly selective. Using Scholastic Aptitude Test (SAT) scores as an index of student academic proficiency, the typical Cornellian places more than 300 points higher than the national average.

In 1964, Cornell set up a Committee on Special Educational Projects (COSEP), with a mission to recruit, assist in admissions, and provide academic, social, and psychological support for minority and disadvantaged students. Over the years, they have been recruited from all parts of the United States, including Puerto Rico; almost half are and have been residents of New York state, and a large percentage are from the New York City metropolitan area. COSEP students' SAT scores average about 150 points lower than those of typical Cornellians. Although it would seem that, as a group, they are better prepared than most students in the nation, at Cornell, their entry-level capabilities and the highly competitive orientation of the other students on campus do not augur well for academic success, particularly in the freshman year.

Other factors also militate against a successful freshman year for COSEP students. They lacked the informal networks that many Cornellians take for granted—tips from alumni relatives, access to fraternity and sorority exam files, acquaintance with a sympathetic faculty member who is known to the family, to mention only a few. Further, although formal and informal counseling were accessible to the general student population, COSEP students found these contacts difficult to arrange and frequently disappointing in their results. A recent campus-based study of minority student advisement revealed that, while advisers felt that they were attuned to the special needs and circumstances of minority students, many students found that advisers were insensitive to their particular circumstances and either unable or unwilling to discuss their personal problems. The unfortunate consequence was that minority students were likely to seek out the relatively few black or Hispanic advisers for supplemental counseling.

Recognizing that many COSEP students would be unable to cope for any length of time without some form of academic assistance, Cornell established a Learning Skills Center to provide them with academic support and personal counseling. Center services are geared to the first two years, since Cornell expects COSEP students to become independent learners by the time they reach the junior year. Little is available to upperclassmen, beyond Learning Skills Center facilities and technical resources. In keeping with its original mandate, the Center concentrates its services on the task of academic foundation building. Its major goal is to give COSEP students the skills and confidence necessary to compete successfully in the classroom.

Some COSEP students make their first contact with the Learning Skills Center through its prefreshman summer program. About one third of each entering COSEP class is required to participate in six weeks of preparatory and introductory courses. These students usually have the weakest high school records; their SAT scores, on the average, are 100 points below those of students who do not attend the summer program. Each student is programmed for a regular credit-bearing university course. He also is required to take a study skills course and two developmental courses, all without credit. The noncredit courses focus on improving skills required for key freshman courses, including biology, chemistry, and mathematics. COSEP students have frequent occasions to meet with advisers who give them much-needed information about university life and about what will be expected of them during the freshman year. Pre- and posttesting in academic areas suggests that these introductory six weeks can be pivotal. Over the years, studies of COSEP students' first-year grades have indicated that, although the summer program students were not as strong as their COSEP peers, their grade point averages after two semesters at Cornell were comparable.

It has already been mentioned that Learning Skills Center activities are almost entirely devoted to helping COSEP students to complete the freshman and sophomore years successfully. During the first year, students are offered a variety of supplemental courses that complement particular core courses in the sciences. Lecturers who hold joint appointments in the Learning Skills Center and in sponsoring academic departments hold special sessions on a weekly basis and review work covered in the classroom. They encourage COSEP students to ask questions. Ordinarily, COSEP students are reluctant to do so. Lecturers also give practice quizzes so that students can monitor their potential in a given course. Their general accessibility in the classroom, combined with their frequent office hours, help COSEP students to compensate for the inequalities in skills levels between themselves and the general student population. Periodic evaluations of Center effectiveness have shown that COSEP students who actively and conscientiously participate in the supplemental instruction program achieve a letter grade improvement in the course or courses involved.

Learning Skills Center services for sophomores are primarily in the form of tutorials. Unlike supplemental instruction courses, which accommodate fifty students or more, tutoring involves single individuals or small groups no larger than five. As sophomores, COSEP students are supposed to be proficient in problem-solving techniques. They generally know what to expect from their professors as regards curricula and examinations. Yet, difficulties arise in understanding key concepts and relating them to other principles in a course. Tutoring sessions, therefore, seek to bridge this gap through explanation, question-and-answer exercises, and demonstration. In the final analysis, tutorials make a tangible difference only to students who are not doing well in a particular course. COSEP students who are performing on a satisfactory level or better would gain little from them. Regular assessments have shown that more than 75 percent of the COSEP students who sign up for tutorials receive a grade of C or better.

A program for reading and study skills improvement has been developed by Learning Skills Center personnel to help COSEP students improve their reading comprehension and speed and to develop effective study habits. Accordingly, the Center sponsors a semesterlong credit-bearing reading improvement course and offers minicourses on study skills improvement. A reading laboratory is available for anyone who would like to do independent work in reading skills. Interestingly, with the passage of years, non-COSEP Cornellians have discovered this service. At present, they account for almost half of the students served by this component of the Learning Skills Center.

Long Island University/Brooklyn Center. Founded a little more than a half century ago, the Brooklyn Center of Long Island University (LIU) is the parent campus of a multicampus private university. Its student body, composed almost exclusively of first-generation collegians, is a microcosm of the New York City metropolitan area population. A significant percentage of the Center's undergraduates can be categorized as minority—black, Hispanic, Asian—but even these terms give no hint of the great diversity of backgrounds and national origins within each group. Nonminority students, mostly of Italian, Irish, or Jewish ancestry, can usually refer to grandparents who were born in the "old country"; quite a few can claim more recent ties to a European past.

During the early 1970s, the Brooklyn Center of Long Island University was directly affected by the open admissions policy mandated for the City University of New York. It began to admit students who had not been adequately prepared for college-level work. Unlike Cornell, where underprepared students, in the aggregate, had SAT scores well above the national average, LIU Brooklyn students who fell into this category had combined scores below 800, and some with scores below 600 were admitted to a special develpmental skills program. A disturbingly large number of entering freshmen had not taken the SAT and were arriving with the General Equivalency Diploma as their sole credential. Perhaps 60 percent were coming directly from the senior year of high school. The others were returning to the educational pursuits after several years away from school.

While the older students were no better prepared than their eighteen- or nineteen-year-old peers, they were more mature and highly directed toward career objectives. Also, they tended to be less resistant to the idea of developmental, compensatory work, although they were more insistent about understanding the rationale for courses and class assignments. The young students, most of whom were graduates of New York City high schools, often appeared immature and without motivation, although many had exaggerated and unrealistic career goals. The transition between high school and college, which lasted only a matter of months, caused a rude shock. Most students probably understood that their preparation for college work had been inadequate, at best; yet, they were not always "ready" for developmental courses and programs. For these students, the strength of their determination was severely tested at their first contact with college. They found the task of catching up a burden in itself.

Brooklyn Center officials were hard put to devise services and programs to accommodate these underprepared students, but by 1974 they had established an Office of Special Academic Services to coordinate all special academic and counseling programs. In a succession of events very similar to those at Cornell, LIU Brooklyn quickly organized a learning center through which many of the compensatory academic support services could be channeled. The overriding concern at both institutions was essentially the same: to concentrate on the basic skills during the two lower division years so that underprepared students would become able to hold their own in the classroom. It is widely perceived at LIU Brooklyn that many students who now complete their baccalaureate degree requirements would fail to do so without these support services and programs. Internal program reviews and federal and state evaluation reports confirm this assessment.

The principal services available to underprepared students at LIU Brooklyn's learning center are individual and small-group tutoring, walk-in workshops, and basic skills laboratories. Assistance is offered for most lower division courses. Not unexpectedly, the greatest demand is for freshman and sophomore English and science courses. Most English tutoring is done on an individual basis, whereas science and mathematics sessions are held for groups of two or three. Walk-in workshops are scheduled, some on a regular biweekly basis, for subjects in very heavy demand. Study skills and math anxiety workshops are also very popular. Over the years, periodic evaluations of the learning center's tutorial services have revealed that students who attend sessions regularly for a period of six weeks or more will improve their course grade by at least one letter grade and sometimes more. Basic skills laboratories have been designed to accompany developmental skills courses in English composition, reading comprehension, and mathematics. The courses are taught on the standard model of lecture and classroom discussion, and there are frequent one-hour examinations. In contrast, the laboratories are completely individualized. Thus, basic skills development is available in two complementary instructional situations.

In a manner consistent with LIU Brooklyn policy, the learning center has become an integral part of a much larger, comprehensive approach to the education of underprepared students. The spectrum of services and programs, of which the learning center is but a part, includes federal and state-funded counseling for underprepared disadvantaged minority students and two university-sponsored developmental skills and freshman guidance programs for underprepared students. All these programs have been very effective in such problem areas as financial aid, lack of motivation, poor self-image, and realistic career goals. Their professional counselors are well aware that deprived family backgrounds and dismal high school environments are at the root of many difficulties that their students face. Learning center staff members, working closely with these program counselors, concentrate on building the academic skills of this student group. However, they are not unaware of the external influences that adversely affect these students and make it difficult for them to cope with the demands of the academic world.

The coordination and cooperation that exist between counselors and learning center staff members have been achieved in a variety of ways. Learning center personnel meet regularly with special program directors to discuss delivery of services and anticipated needs. An academic resources committee composed of learning center staff, special program counselors, and library professionals is responsible for selection of materials, evaluation of students' progress in reading and mathematics, integration of audiovisual aids into developmental courses and skills laboratories, and extension of learning center services to community groups outside the university. Faculty members are encouraged to refer their students to the learning center for work on English grammer, term paper assignments, and research projects. They may, and do, request workshops on topics and areas in which their students are having difficulty. In a way that complements the efforts of the learning center staff, a number of faculty members have volunteered for retraining in order to teach developmental skills courses in reading and mathematics. Their awareness of learning center–related issues has been enormously helpful in broadening support among the LIU Brooklyn community for its academic and counseling supportive services.

Areas of Common Concern

The two learning centers described in this chapter have clearly been successful in helping underprepared students to improve their academic performance levels and to become better adjusted to the competitive atmosphere of the college campus. It has already been noted that many of these students need more than regular academic assistance. Students with serious psychological problems, personal problems, or both must be referred to appropriate campus counseling services. If such services do not exist or if on-campus counseling resources are limited, learning center staff can use listings of community services to make outside referrals. Still, the learning center can be very effective in helping students to adjust to campus life and understand its competitive nature. The following paragraphs discuss some adjustment problems that these students have and some ideas that the authors have for possible solutions.

Student Anxiety. Underprepared students usually approach the learning center in an anxious frame of mind. Having never had much success in school, they wonder if this is not the final step toward yet another failure. Such questions as "Why am I doing this?" and "Do I really belong here?" are uppermost in their minds. They think that their peers in the classroom are smarter, better attuned to the course curriculum, and far more likely to earn better grades. In this frame of mind, it is little wonder that they sometimes appear negative and suspicious. If learning center staff members are sensitive to these students' hesitancy and sense of inadequacy they can do much to help them to overcome their anxieties.

First encounters—with admissions officers and other campus officials, with classroom instructors, and with learning center staff—can directly affect how a student reacts to the entire university setting. Students should find the learning center a comfortable place to be. If they find all sorts of other students on hand as they look around, they will be reassured. Learning center personnel should be able to see through the suspicious attitudes, moroseness, insistent demands for services, and complaints about instructors, courses, and university offices and decide how much can be ascribed to the student's feeling of inadequacy and anxiety and how much to fact. One very frequent source of anxiety arises from a student's very real fear of a particular subject. Perhaps poor teaching methods had been used in the elementary school, or the student had been humiliated in class, or a teacher had made distinctions between how girls and boys should be taught. These are only a few of the reasons why an undergraduate can feel anxious when exposed to the subject in college. Mathematics is a major source of difficulty, but students can have emotional blocks about any subject. Since underprepared students are especially prone to anxiety problems, learning center personnel should be trained, through orientation workshops and exposure to the literature, to help their students to cope with and overcome their fears.

One very effective way of putting underprepared students at ease, which requires little expenditure of energy and in which the students themselves will make the necessary associations, is to have individuals on the learning center staff who can serve as role models. The typical university community has few faculty members or administrators of racial or ethnic minority background. The learning center should be more representative, both because it is relatively new on campus and can reflect the changed social attitudes of the last two decades and because underprepared students will not have positive feelings about their situation if all learning center staff members are from one group and all the students are from another. If these considerations are taken into account, students will find role models where they will, among the center's tutors, instructors, or administrative personnel. They will try to internalize many of the traits they see displayed, since possession of the traits obviously has paid off for others.

Student Expectations. Underprepared students often aspire to professions about which they know very little. Their expectations may be completely discordant with the realities of course requirements, choices of departmental majors, and the many other hurdles that must be cleared before the long-sought professional status has been attained. Experience with underprepared student populations at Cornell and the Brooklyn Center underscores this. These students at once underestimate the competitive environment of the college campus and overestimate their chances of success in competitive academic situations. Students who have such a picture suffer a rude awakening almost from their very first day on campus.

Students' first need is to know what to expect in any given course— what kinds of examinations will be given, what additional assignments will be made, how the instructor intends to determine the final grade. All too often, the first examination of the semester is also the first glimpse that students have of what will be required as the semester progresses. A low grade on the first test will demoralize some students to the point where they lose all confidence. Learning centers are well suited to helping such students adjust their expectations about college work so that there will be more congruence between their expectations and experiences. Approaches that work include practice quizzes, supplementary courses, additional laboratory work, and skills workshops attuned to specific courses. Any one of them, or a combination thereof, will help students to evaluate their situation in a more realistic framework. Although the process may still be painful, some of the agony, demoralization, and frustration will be gone.

Student Responsibility. Many underprepared students, particularly those from inner-city schools, arrive on campus with little or no ability to deal with structured situations. Unwittingly, it would seem, they have opted to compete in one of the most demanding and tightly structured environments possible. Their previous secondary school background or their absence from school for some years makes it unlikely that they will succeed unless they understand clearly that certain kinds of responsible behavior will be required of them. Most exhibit one or more of the following characteristics: unawareness of the need to be punctual for class, inconsistency in class attendance, inability to take usable lecture notes, poor textbook reading techniques. These inadequacies must be remedied before students can be expected to show significant academic progress. Somehow, the entire spectrum of campus agencies, programs, and services has to cooperate in helping students to change these behavioral patterns. An individual special admit program, counseling service, or learning center will not be able to do it alone.

Learning centers can foster student responsibility. Indeed, that should be considered one of their primary responsibilities. At LIU Brooklyn, for instance, where many of the underprepared students fit the profile just drawn, the learning center's major tutorial services offering takes the form of contract tutoring. Prior to the first meeting, each student signs a contract, which is countersigned by the tutor. Thereafter, the student is obliged to attend regularly, until he formally indicates that he no longer wishes assistance. This contract system reflects a conscious effort to instill a greater sense of responsibility in students who use the service. While the system is not so formal as to deter students, it does encourage them to keep appointments. Students do not relate to their tutors as if they were instructors, but they certainly do not relate to them as fellow students who are being met for social reasons. Students arrive for sessions, sign in, and proceed to assigned carrels to work with their appointed tutors. Most have reacted positively to the professional atmosphere of the tutoring center, and their ability to keep appointments has improved markedly over the years. On the whole, tutoring is taken very seriously. The "rap session" occurs infrequently, and on the rare occasions when tutors have encouraged such informality, the students invariably have complained that they were not being helped.

Independent Learning. Perhaps the most valuable effect that the learning center can have is to improve the underprepared student's attitude toward learning in the college or university setting. Learning is an active process; it involves practice and experience. An anxious student who lacks family or academic role models or a student with inappropriate expectations about college is apt to be a passive learner—one who tries to absorb information without participating actively in its organization and synthesis. Passive learning is incompatible with success because it leads to poor study habits and a general inability to prepare for assignments and examinations. It also fosters dependence. And, herein lies a serious threat to the effectiveness of learning centers. Utmost care must be taken to avoid a crisis intervention atmosphere so that students will not think of the learning center only as the place to go in an emergency. The greatest service that these centers can perform for underprepared students is to make them better informed about and more involved in the actual learning process. Only then will they be independent learners, capable of mastering what is expected of them as they move from one course to another.

Conclusions

Academic readiness has become a national issue. Popular magazines and daily newspapers routinely carry articles in which the general decline in student skills is pointed to as the sign of a deeply-rooted educational malaise. The academic skills courses and compensatory services that were once reserved for the underprepared students discussed in this chapter are no longer the exclusive preserve of the students. This development, however, should offer little comfort to those who have been working with underprepared students. The numbers of underprepared students are increasing, while secondary school preparation remains as inadequate as ever. Socioeconomic pressures continue to weigh heavily on students' families and neighborhoods. As their ranks swell, the problem of providing effective assistance will be exacerbated. Resources are already stretched dangerously thin, and generous infusions of supplementary funds are unlikely to materialize in the immediate future. Indeed, the 1980s may be the decade in which Americans will decide whether to support the liberal traditions of the previous two decades or to eliminate the funding on which so many students and academic support programs have depended.

In this changing academic and fiscal environment, the learning center is being asked to extend its services to all students who need academic assistance. At the same time, it cannot reduce or dilute its services to underprepared students. But, as its services become more inclusive and as new student groups begin to use its service, the learning center will find itself more highly regarded within the academic community. In the past, there has been a general reluctance to view its activities as anything other than remedial in nature. If learning center administrators can seize the initiative and adapt their support services to the needs of all students, the chances for complete integration of the learning center into the structure of higher education will increase immeasurably. Continued administrative support and survival as a campus institution both seem to hinge directly on this outreach to the entire student body. Predictably, underprepared students will regard learning centers in a more positive way. No longer will they need to ask "What am I doing here?" They will have only to look around to discover that they are not alone.

References

Centra, J. A. "Reading the Enrollment Barometer." *Change*, 1979, *11* (3), 50–62.
Chambers, M. M. "Higher Education's Future: Much Brighter Than You May Think." *Chronicle of Higher Education*, August 25, 1980, p. 72.

"Cornell Indicators." Office of Institutional Planning and Analysis, Cornell University, January 1980, p. 7.

Cross, K. P. *Beyond the Open Door: New Students to Higher Education.* San Francisco: Jossey-Bass, 1971.

Cross, K. P. *Accent on Learning: Improving Instruction and Reshaping the Curriculum.* San Francisco: Jossey-Bass, 1976.

Enright, G., and Kerstiens, G. "The Learning Center: Toward an Expanded Role." In O. Lenning and R. Nayman (Eds.), *New Directions for College Learning Assistance: New Roles for Learning Assistance,* no. 2. San Francisco: Jossey-Bass, 1980.

Frances, C. "Apocalyptic Versus Strategic Planning." *Change,* 1980, *12* (5), 19–44.

Geiger, R. S. "The Case of the Missing Students." *Change,* 1978, *10* (9), 64–65.

Harris, M., and Fisher, J. "Modeling and Flexiblity in Problem Solving." *Psychological Reports,* 1973, *33,* 19–23.

Hedegard, J. M., and Brown, D. R. "Negro and White Freshmen at a Public Multiuniversity." *Psychological Reports,* 1973, *33,* 19–33.

Karwin, J. J. *Flying Learning Center: Design and Costs of an Off-Campus Space for Learning.* Berkeley, Calif.: Carnegie Commission on Higher Education, 1973.

Maxwell, M. J. "Learning Style and Other Correlates of Gains in Scanning Speed." *Journal of Reading Behavior,* 1978, *10,* 49–56.

Maxwell, M. J. *Improving Student Learning Skills: A Comprehensive Guide to Successful Practices and Programs for Increasing the Performance of Underprepared Students.* San Francisco: Jossey-Bass, 1979.

Myers, C. "Verbal, Math SAT Scores Decline to All-Time Low." *Chronicle of Higher Education,* September 17, 1979, *19* (3).

Peterson, G. T. *The Learning Center.* Hamden, Conn.: Shoe String Press, 1975.

Reed, R. *Peer-Tutoring Programs for the Academically Deficient Student in Higher Education.* Berkeley, Calif.: Center for Research and Development in Higher Education, 1974.

Richards, C. S. "Behavior Modification of Studying Through Study Skills Advice and Self-Control Procedures." *Journal of Counseling Psychology,* 1975, *22* (5), 431–436.

Rossman, J. E., and others. *Open Admissions at the City University of New York: An Analysis of the First Year.* Englewood Cliffs, N.J.: Prentice-Hall, 1975.

Sullivan, L. L. *A Guide to Higher Education Learning Centers in the United States and Canada.* Portsmouth, N.H.: Entelek, 1977.

Tobias, S. *Overcoming Math Anxiety.* Boston: Houghton Mifflin, 1978.

Voeks, V. *On Becoming an Educated Person.* Philadelphia: Saunders, 1970.

Yates, J. F., and Collins, W. "Self-Confidence and Motivation Among Black and White College Freshmen: An Exploration." In A. W. Boykin and others (Eds.), *Research Directions of Black Psychologists.* New York: Basic Books, 1979.

Yates, J. F., Collins, W., and Boykin, A. W. "Some Approaches to Black Academic Motivation in Predominantly White Universities." *Journal of Social and Behavioral Sciences,* 1974, *20* (3), 19–37.

Yates, J. F., and Meyers, S. D. "Subjective Probabilities of Competitive Success: General Levels, Relationships to Task Values, and Racial Comparisons." Unpublished manuscript, University of Michigan, 1973.

*William Collins is director of the Learning Skills
Center at Cornell University in Ithaca, New
York. The author of "Developing Basic Skills
Through Learning Center Summer Programs,"
an article that appeared in Serving
Underprepared Students (ACT Program, 1981),
he is engaged in research on prediction of
underprepared student achievement.*

*Lester Wilson is director of Special
Academic Services at the Brooklyn Center of
Long Island University.*

The quality of services for handicapped students in postsecondary education is a barometer of institutional strength and vitality.

Handicapped Students in the Learning Center

Nicholas J. Hirtz

Until recent years, handicapped students in postsecondary education had to depend on their own initiative or on the limited, voluntary efforts of a few widely scattered colleges and universities to meet their needs. Congress did create semipublic corporations, such as Gallaudet College and the National Institute for the Deaf, located on the campus of the Rochester Institute of Technology, to further the education of students with severe hearing impairments. However, the great majority of handicapped students was still not afforded an equal opportunity in any area of postsecondary education.

The Rehabilitation Act of 1973 (Public Law 93-112, Section 504, Subpart E) was the first federal civil rights law to protect the rights of handicapped persons and reflect a national commitment to end discrimination on the basis of handicap. Section 504, Subpart E prohibits any such prejudicial action by educational programs and activities that receive federal financial assistance. Department of Health, Education, and Welfare (DHEW) regulations for the implementation of Section 504 were published in the *Federal Register,* on May 4, 1977, and they became effective on June 3, 1977.

Definition. The DHEW regulations define a handicapped person as "anyone who has a physical or mental impairment which substantially

L. Wilson (Ed.). *New Directions for College Learning Assistance: Helping Special Student Groups,* no. 7. San Francisco: Jossey-Bass, March 1982.

limits one or more major life activities, has a record of such an impairment, or is regarded as having such an impairment" (84.3.j). The regulations also define a handicapped person "qualified" for postsecondary and vocational education as a "handicapped individual who meets academic and technical standards requisite to admission or participation in the education program or activity" (84.3.k,3).

It is important to emphasize that these regulations apply not only to physical handicaps but also to mental impairments, such as mental retardation, organic brain syndrome, emotional or mental illness, and specific learning disabilities. It should also be remembered that a handicapped person must be "qualified" for entry or participation in the education program or activity.

Parameters. While the DHEW regulations prohibit discrimination on the basis of handicap in all education programs and activities that receive federal financial assistance, four regulations have direct impact on learning centers on college and university campuses.

First, programs and activities shall be operated in the "most integrated setting appropriate" (84.43,d). The most integrated setting appropriate is usually referred to as the *mainstream.* Second, modifications shall be made to ensure that the academic requirements "do not discriminate or have the effect of discriminating." Examples of these modifications are course substitutions, when possible, extension of time for assignments, alternate methods of administering examinations, and increased individualization of instruction. Academic requirements that can be demonstrated as essential to the program or course of instruction will not be regarded as discriminatory (84.44,a). Third, course examinations shall measure achievement rather than reflect the student's impaired sensory, manual, or speaking skills, "except where such skills are the factors the test purports to measure" (84.44,c). Fourth, steps shall be taken, as necessary, to ensure that "no handicapped individual is denied the benefits of, excluded from participation in, or otherwise subjected to discrimination under the education program or activity because of the absence of auxiliary aids for students with impaired sensory, manual, or speaking skills." Examples of auxiliary aids are taped texts, interpreters, and readers for the visually impaired (84.44,d).

Funding. Congress did not provide direct funding for the implementation of Section 504. Expenses, therefore, for academic modifications, auxiliary aids, removal of physical barriers, and staff to administer programs for the handicapped must be covered by the institution's budget, from federal or state categorical grants, which themselves are few in number and specific in purpose, or by private or community resources. The absence of direct funding, however, does not set aside the mandates of the DHEW regulations. Creativity, imagination, and judicious use of available resources can take most colleges and universities a long way toward compliance with Section 504.

Assistance. It has already been noted that the DHEW regulations are comprehensive and mandatory for all institutions that receive federal funds. In order to achieve compliance, however, institutions that so desire can obtain assistance from the Office for Civil Rights, from educational associations in Washington or in various state capitals, from state departments of education, and from trained consultants and directors of model programs.

Population and Potential

Approximately 36,000,000 Americans are handicapped under DHEW definitions. About 28,000,000 adults fall into this category. Of this number approximately 12 percent may be prospective students in post-secondary education.

Recent studies have found that only .5 percent of the students enrolled in colleges and universities in the fall of 1978 were handicapped and that most of the students were in public two-year institutions ("Handicapped Students Favor Two-Year Colleges," 1980). In Florida, in the same year, the combined enrollment of handicapped students from twenty-eight (of thirty-seven) reporting institutions was 3,707. The average number of handicapped students per public institution was 133. Seventy percent of these students were in community colleges. Full-time student status was reported for 63 percent of these students (Special Education and Rehabilitation Systems, 1981).

It is safe to conclude that handicapped students are grossly underrepresented in higher education. However, the reasons for their reluctance or inability to attend colleges are not easily determined. Severity of the handicapping condition, lack of conviction in the ability of institutions to meet their needs, and limited counseling and recruiting efforts are factors that contribute to the low enrollment figures.

As an institution improves its capacity to serve the handicapped and as it gains visibility in the network of services provided for the members of this group, enrollments will increase. At Miami-Dade Community College's South Campus, where an organized program for the handicapped was initiated in the fall of 1978, an informal headcount revealed a student enrollment of 120. Two years later, even after 30 students were removed from the original roster because they did not qualify as handicapped, there were 150 disabled students on campus. In the nation as a whole, with the support of newly organized efforts to give this group greater access to higher education, all indicators point to a steady increase in their numbers during the 1980s.

In line with this trend, experience at Miami-Dade South has shown that handicapped students are showing greater variation in disability type and increased severity level. Perhaps 50 percent have a physical or visual impairment. The rest evidence a wide variety of disability categories. A small percentage will have a hearing impairment. Others are learning disabled, or they have seizure disorders or an emotional disability. Indeed, the learning disabled accounted for 20 percent of the entire handicapped student population, and one of the strongest requests at a regional meeting in Miami in 1980 on the needs of handicapped students was for a program to accommodate the learning-disabled college student (Special Education and Rehabilitation Systems, 1981).

In the future, therefore, we can anticipate a growing number of disabled students and greater diversity in their handicapping conditions. The use of taped texts and the provision of readers, interpreters, and various other auxiliary aids—without doubt the easiest of all services to offer—will accommodate only about 50 percent of these students. What will prove effective for the other 50 percent, particularly the mentally impaired?

Systems of Support Services

Academic and counseling support for disabled students depends on the institution's system for the delivery of services to students and on the models used to build the program. Several different delivery systems and models can be identified, although they do not always operate in as mutually exclusive a manner as the following descriptions may suggest.

Independent. Some students either do not regard themselves as handicapped or refuse to use special equipment or services. Others seek academic and counseling support exclusively from outside sources, from family, friends, and community agencies. If these students survive and are able to cope with the rigors of college life, no valid concerns about their welfare should arise. Of course, crises and emergencies will sometimes occur. In such instances, as campus personnel who deal with handicapped students can attest, students who have not previously been identified as disabled will be so designated as a result of their need for academic assistance, counseling, or both. It should be remembered, nevertheless, that the independent student is not as rare as might be expected.

Extreme Mainstream. This term is euphemistically applied to situations in which college and university support systems for handicapped students are almost totally nonexistent. This unfortunate state of affairs is legal, if not moral, for institutions that receive no federal financial assistance. The extreme mainstream varies in degree, of course, but ultimately it obliges disabled students to use the delivery systems designed for traditional students, to drop out of school altogether, or to seek admission to a college or university that can meet their needs.

Modified Mainstream. The modified mainstream differs from the extreme mainstream situation in that students are afforded a limited choice of services, which are presented in an informal way. What is offered is unorganized and not backed up by a budget or by assigned staff members. The students receive assistance individually on an ad hoc basis, in direct relation to the pressure of their demands and their visibility. Often, a volunteer or a group of volunteers, usually from the student services area, will attempt to provide services in an informal and unsystematic way. A committee may eventually be formed to determine the needs and special requirements of disabled students and to gain the support of the administration. Under ordinary conditions, the modified mainstream can be somewhat effective, especially if all parties concerned are working toward the elaboration of a comprehensive and coordinated mainstream model.

Comprehensive and Coordinated Mainstream. The strength of the comprehensive and coordinated mainstream model lies in its well-defined plan, its budget, the presence of responsible staff members with authority, and its administrative support. Historically, many of the programs that can be categorized by this term have spun off from student services areas and evolved into units with slightly different structures and considerably more independence. This model allows the handicapped student to function in the mainstream of academic life through special services delivered under the same system that is in operation for other students. The students themselves may or may not be organized into a disabled students program, but the delivery system built on this model functions effectively in either case. Since it depends on the delivery of services to disabled students through the institution's regular support systems, the comprehensive mainstream requires that personnel in the support and instructional systems know how to deal with the disabled students who will ask for their help. If there is a disabled student services unit or program on campus, its personnel can be used to train and support their colleagues in the comprehensive mainstream system. If there is not, some formal training will have to be given, or the system will founder altogether. In summation, disabled students will find that this particular model provides equal opportunity and accessibility within a single framework, which usually is cost-effective as well.

Ghetto. The ghetto is a microcosm of the college or university in which it is found. Disabled students are recruited, admitted, registered, counseled, tutored, instructed, and offered a miscellany of other support services—all directed to their particular group. The ghetto delivery system, which is usually housed in the developmental, counseling, or learning center areas, is characteristically a distinct department or section, although it is not always completely self-contained. The most common example of program outreach to a mainstream activity is in classroom instruction. This model does have some advantages. It is highly visible to the personnel of the institution, to its students, and to the community at large; it is directly accountable for its services and budgetary expenditures; and, most importantly, it is able to deliver services. The disadvantages of this system lie in its violation of the principle of the "most integrated setting appropriate," in the dependence that it creates among disabled students, who will not have similar services at their disposal after they graduate or leave the academic setting, and finally in high costs associated wth trained personnel and separate services.

Special Program/Special Institution. Individual institutions, regional centers, and semipublic corporations have created special programs and courses of study for specific categories of disabilities, especially for the deaf. Examples of such programs include the St. Petersburg Junior College (Florida) Secretarial Careers for the Deaf program, the vocational programs at the regional center for the deaf at Delgado Community College in New Orleans, and the liberal arts programs at Gallaudet College in Washington, D.C. Specific programs like these rely heavily on federal aid, except in strictly vocational education, which is sometimes funded partially by the state.

The disadvantages of the ghetto model are also evident in the special programs for students with specific handicaps and in the regional and federal centers for disabled students. However, these programs and centers are not the answer to the needs of the entire handicapped population, nor were they ever intended to be. In addition, the existence of predetermined courses of study for specific categories of disability and the limited career choices offered to disabled students both hint of paternalism. Finally, these students frequently have to leave home in order to take advantage of the special programs. This is not a fortunate alternative, because of the expense involved, strong family and social ties, and the physical inconvenience. In the state of Florida, for instance, 59 percent of the disabled students chose their college because of its proximity to home (Special Education and Rehabilitation Systems, 1981). The negative aspects of special programs and institutions are not presented here to deny either their need and/or their ultimate contributions. The point is that a student should have access to a wide variety of educational alternatives and not be limited to any one category of service delivery.

Learning Centers and Disabled Students

Because the learning center offers academic support services to the general student population, it can be added to this list of educational alternatives for disabled students. As such, it must be completely accessible, which means that many procedures and techniques for delivering services may have to be adapted in order to suit the distinctive needs of disabled students. Other, more specialized strategies and interventions should become familiar to learning center staff members as well. For all these adjustments to the routine patterns of working with nondisabled students to lead to success, the active participation and support of the college or university administration, the director of the learning center, and the entire learning center staff are required.

To give some idea of the dimensions of the problem, it is appropriate here to present some hypothetical descriptions of disabled students who could easily be among the daily visitors to any learning center:

Marilyn is a very gifted upper sophomore. A student in the college science honors program, she has excelled in every science and mathematics course that she has taken thus far, and she has a cumulative A- average. This semester, Marilyn is taking an English course that requires a lengthy, analytical term paper. Although she has not had much difficulty with earlier English courses, the term paper assignment has brought her to the learning center in search of assistance. Marilyn has cerebral palsy. It is very difficult to understand her words and phrases. As a result of her lack of coordination, she cannot focus on written material for more than a few minutes at a time, which necessitates that much of it be read to her. How will the learning center staff member who is assigned to work with Marilyn best assist with the term paper, in light of her severe physical handicap? How will the two comfortably communicate with each other?

John has just begun his first semester in college. He did not come from an academically rigorous high school. In fact, he is very weak in the basic skills, particularly in mathematics. His placement test results reflected these deficiencies, so his counselor had no other choice but to assign him to an almost complete schedule of developmental courses. John quickly realized that the most elementary computaton was extremely difficult for him, and he, too, found his way to he learning center in search of a tutor. John is blind. How will the peer tutor who will work with John manage to help him with the abstractions and highly visual nature of mathematics?

From his earliest recollection, Louis had always aspired to go to law school and become a lawyer like his father. His SAT scores were very respectable, and he was able to enter a very prestigious state university as a prelaw major. During his first semester on campus, Louis was required to take a public speaking course. Louis is deaf, and he quickly found himself in trouble. He decided to go to the learning center to see if he could get some help. On his way, he stopped at the disabled student services office to see if Jan, his sign language interpreter, was free. She was, and the two of them continued on to the learning center. How will the language specialist be able to assist Louis? The presence of Jan means that he will not have to know sign language, but he will still have to know something about the special language needs of deaf students, will he not?

The foregoing hypothetical cases underscore the great diversity of handicapping conditions and the extreme range of academic preparaton levels and skills that are to be found in the disabled student population of any school. The following paragraphs will discuss the delivery of learning center services to this student group in terms of component elements. If these elements are brought together systematically and rationally, they will make these new campus institutions a viable educational alternative for handicapped students.

Mission. It is well recognized that the mission of the learning center is to provide reinforcement for nontraditional academic activities. The professionals who control the direction of these centers should consider how this mission statement applies to the handicapped students on campus and to their centers' human resources and facilities. Once the scope of services has been delineated, the organizational structure, technology, and staff capabilities should be carefully reviewed to ensure that all available resources are being used as effectively as possible.

The most frequent organizational situation is one in which the learning center director does not have the authority or resources to provide a full-scale battery of services for disabled students. A comprehensive institutional network, of which the learning center is only a part, albeit the pivotal one, is the preferred structural arrangement. To this purpose, the administration should create a full-time position for the coordination of existing disabled student services, if there is not already such a person on campus. The coordinator, who should have a graduate degree in educational psychology, will assist the learning center in developing and refining its delivery capabilities. Within this framework of cooperation and sharing of resources, the disabled student services coordinator can also be expected to offer in-service training seminars and workshops to learning center staff members and peer tutors.

Administrative Support. Learning centers cannot exist in isolation from the college or university administration, nor should their personnel hesitate to work closely with other student support systems on campus. Top-level administrative backing for the delivery of learning center services to disabled students is of paramount importance, but it should extend to the entire gamut of student services systems, ranging from recruitment and admissions to academic programs and counseling offices. In the final analysis, administrative decisions will determine whether the institution establishes a separate support system or opts to incorporate its disabled students into existing support services and programs.

Staff Training. The ability of a learning center to provide effective assistance to disabled students will always be inextricably related to the sensitivity and professonal training found in the center's counseling and instructional staff. As already noted, a campus disabled students coordinator is extremely desirable. This person should offer sustained instruction in strategies and techniques useful in helping this student group. In some cases, the center already has a staff member who is capable of guiding his learning center colleagues. In others, it does not. In either situation, the need for enlightenment is urgent. Learning centers and other campus organizations will not succeed with disabled students if they do not have the requisite knowledge, skills, and sensitivity.

Problems related to attitude are a major source of interpersonal difficulties for learning center personnel. The person who is designated to assist staff members in working with disabled students should place a high priority on attitudinal awareness. Professionals, peer tutors, secretaries, and student aides should all be urged to take a close look at their feelings and thoughts about handicapped students. Fortunately, there are ways of facilitating this kind of inward examination. Under the leadership and direction of the disabled student services specialist or of some other person who has suitable training and experience, an informal, pressure-free series of exploratory discussions can be arranged to afford learning center personnel the opportunity to express their concerns and discomforts as well as their positive feelings about working with disabled students. Staff members can be offered a chance to have their interaction with disabled students observed by the specialist. It may even be possible to videotape and evaluate an interaction in a non-threatening way. Tutors can be invited to participate in small-group sessions that include role playing and physical disability simulations. Disabled students can be encouraged to join these sessions when it is clear that participants will not feel threatened by the interaction (Nathanson, 1982). These are only a few of the possibilities that can help to ease the strain and feelings of inadequacy among learning center personnel who are uncomfortable because they do not know what is "right" to say or do.

As for hard, practical information on ways of helping students with specific disabilities, the qualified specialist will have to offer sustained training to center staff and peer tutors. This training should address such questions as these: How do you communicate with a deaf person if you do not know sign language? How do you guide a blind person to a seat, past an obstacle, through a doorway, or across a street? How do you communicate with a person who has severely impaired speech? How can you determine whether a student really does need assistance, and what is the best way of providing it?

As these questions are being discussed, learning center staff members should be given information on specific disabling conditions, on existing supportive services on campus and in neighboring communities, and on the special appliances and equipment already in place and ready for use. Staff need a list of the locations and telephone numbers of colleagues who have worked with disabled students and who can provide practical advice. Finally, staff should also have easy access to a representative sampling of the literature on specific disabilities. A wealth of free information is available. The reader may wish to consult the following: *The College Student with a Disability: A Faculty Handbook*, distributed by the President's Committee on Employment of the Handicapped; *Teaching Chemistry to Physically Handicapped Students*, prepared by the American Chemical Society; and the *Handbook for the Blind College Student*, published by the National Federation of the Blind. The suggestions offered here and in preceding paragraphs should help learning center staff members to feel more at ease with the disabled students who come to them for help and better prepared to respond to them.

Technology. Equipment that serves as auxiliary aids for handicapped students is available now, and it has improved rapidly in recent years. Even equipment designed for nonhandicapped consumers can be put to use. For example, the tape recorder can obviate the need for blind and other visually impaired students to take notes during lectures and classes. Another example is the electric typewriter, which a student with poor motor control can use if a few touch control adaptations are made.

Sometimes, a mouth stick will be the adaptation needed. Other times, attaching a raised metal ring around the edge of each key will make it possible for a student to use this machine. At Miami-Dade South, for instance, microcomputers are utilized extensively to assist blind, deaf, and learning-disabled students. Microcomputers project information on television monitors and over voice output units; they also print hard copy. Deaf students can watch the television monitor and read the copy, blind students can listen to information conveyed by the voice output unit or have the hard copy read by a reader, and learning-disabled students may find it helpful to try all three (Hirtz, 1980).

Although a great deal can be done to assist handicapped students with "traditional" equipment, it is encouraging to know that there are also many pieces of equipment designed for specific disabilities on the market. They include print enlargers, talking calculators, variable-speed tape recorders and players, electric page turners, and communication devices for the deaf. It is not always easy to determine where this equipment should be located on campus or where it should be placed in the learning center, unless its function is so specific as to leave no choice. Ultimately, location and placement depend on the purpose of the machine or mechanical aid, the number and relative expense of the equipment involved, its frequency of use, whether it is essential to more than one special program, and the difficulty of moving it from one place to another.

Smaller items, low in cost, portable, and in frequent demand, can be purchased in sufficient numbers to allow them to be placed in several areas—the library, the audiovisual department, the advisement office—and made available to students for school or home use. Tape recorders, magnifying glasses, and talking calculators are examples of this type of equipment. The key concept is to put each piece in an area where it supports student academic activities as conveniently and practically as possible.

Very special equipment—items that are relatively expensive, difficult to move, and infrequently used—presents a more complicated problem. A typical example is the Visualtek machine. Visualtek is the trade name of a closed circuit television system that enlarges print on a television screen. A desk model costs in the neighborhood of $2,500, it is easy to damage when it is moved, and it is of use only to a portion of visually impaired students. Yet, this machine is clearly needed in at least two locations where visually impaired students must read printed materials, the library and the learning center.

Of course, traditional and special equipment cannot substitute for or replace human services. Readers, interpreters, notetakers, and tutors will always be in demand. The preferred situation, clearly, is one in which learning center staff members are available for academic assistance and counseling—services that only humans can offer—and in which disabled students also have access to a variety of auxiliary aids that extend the sensory and motor skills in ways that are possible only through technology.

Comprehensiveness. The most effective system for service delivery is the comprehensive learning assistance program that serves a diverse college or university population and functions in close cooperation with the other support systems on campus. The comprehensiveness of disabled student support services is determined by several variables, including administrative support, a well-defined plan of program operation, a budget, responsible and trained professional staff, developed strategies on practical ways of assisting disabled students, and the size and needs of the student population involved. The reader should realize that the breadth of services described in the preceding paragraphs will not be found on many campuses at this time. It can be hoped, however, that the material presented here will be used as a framework for future development.

The 1980s

In any comparison of handicapped students and more traditional students, the significant variable is that the former will usually require academic modifications and auxiliary aids in order to compete successfully with the latter. If longitudinal studies on grade distribution, retention and attrition rates, graduation, and employment exist for disabled students, their results have not been widely disseminated. Some quantified results are available from the few institutions that have programs for specific categories of disability, but there is very little scholarly work in the literature on the subject of disabled students in the mainstream. The information that does exist is mostly of an anecdotal nature, consisting largely of success stories about individuals who overcame handicaps to become lawyers, doctors, teachers, and media and business world professionals. Nonetheless, it seems safe to conclude that the handicapped student will do as well in college as his nonimpaired peer if he is given a supportive academic environment.

The ability and performance levels of disabled students are determined by college and university admissions standards. Institutions that require high SAT scores and academic competencies make the same demands of disabled students as they make of all other students. Therefore, the handicapped student who enters such an institution has already demonstrated his potential, and he can be expected to perform on a par with the others. In institutions with an open-door admissions policy, the situation depends on the openness of admissions regulations and on the procedures used for student advisement. Will a college with an open-door admissions policy allow students with mental impairments to enroll and take a sequence of developmental courses? What happens when a student is discovered to have moderate or severe learning problems? For more than a decade now, a considerable number of colleges and universities across the country have struggled to respond to the needs of physically disabled students. The advent of "qualified" mentally impaired students adds a further dimension to the problem. If both groups are to be offered a responsive and supportive academic environment further changes in thinking and in delivery systems for disabled students will have to occur. Herein lies a great challenge for college and university learning centers and their academic and counseling support services.

In conclusion, handicapped students are still numerically under-represented on campus, but their enrollments are increasing, as is the diversity among the students themselves. The full effects of the federal regulations on equal opportunity for handicapped students have not yet been realized. New developments and improvements in technical hardware and software are constantly appearing on the market. Funding for services for these students in some areas is beginning to surface at the state level. It is unclear how the severe cutbacks in federal spending will affect the financial support for students and programs that was a hallmark of the 1970s. Nevertheless, learning centers, and particularly their academic support sections, will continue to play a pivotal role in assisting disabled students.

References

Department of Health, Education, and Welfare. *Federal Register.* Title 45, Subtitle A, Part 84. Washington, D.C.: Department of Health, Education, and Welfare, May 4, 1977.

"Handicapped Students Favor Two-Year Colleges." *The Chronicle of Higher Education*, February 11, 1980, p. 17.

Hirtz, N. J. "Equal Opportunity for Handicapped Students in Florida." Paper presented at the National Council on Community Services and Continuing Education, Danvers, Mass., October, 1980.

Nathanson, R. B. "An Exploratory-Descriptive Study of Faculty Attitudes Toward Physically Disabled Students with Proposals for Faculty Development Programming." Unpublished doctoral dissertation, Teachers College, Columbia University, 1982.

Special Education and Rehabilitation Systems. "Needs Assessment and Master Action Plan for Providing a Uniform and Coordinated Delivery System for Handicapped Students Attending Public and Community Colleges and State Universities." Washington, D.C.: Special Education and Rehabilitation Systems, 1981.

*Nicholas J. Hirtz, coordinator of services for
the handicapped at Miami-Dade Community
College, South Campus, from 1978 to 1981,
is the director of legislative liaison and public
affairs at Hillsborough Community College
in Tampa, Florida.*

*The Learning Opportunities Center of Kingsborough
Community College has developed a model
for college survival that is helpful not only
to learning-disabled students but to underprepared
students in general.*

Delivering Services to the
Learning Disabled:
A Holistic Approach

*Irwin Rosenthal
Elaine Fine
Robert de Vight*

Learning-disabled college students are faced with the same varied and
difficult developmental tasks as other young adult collegians. They are
expected to improve their level of cognitive functioning, to achieve independence from family, to prepare for a career, and to develop mature
social relationships and skills. However, many students with learning
disabilities need individualized attention and special support services in
order to fulfill their educational aspirations. To meet the needs of these
special students and to enable them to function effectively in college, a
massive and multifaceted effort is necessary. It must be holistic in nature
and address both the cognitive and affective elements of students' lives. It
must focus on issues related not only to the college environment but to
family and peer relationships as well.

      Typically, learning-disabled young adults have a history of aca-
demic failure. They suffer from social isolation in school as well as in
their neighborhoods and communities. Many are deficient in one or more

L. Wilson (Ed.). *New Directions for College Learning Assistance:
Helping Special Student Groups*, no. 7. San Francisco: Jossey-Bass, March 1982.

of the basic skills. They have come to feel that they make only a minimal impact on their world, and they usually perceive this impact as negative. In short, these students have become the embodiment of Seligman's concept of learned helplessness (Hiroto and Seligman, 1975), for they have learned from the repeated experience of misunderstanding and frustration that their efforts at mastery, both in and out of school, will lead to failure.

As for their preparation for college-level work, many learning-disabled students are found to have severe difficulties in reading comprehension, writing, spelling, and mathematics. They can also have problems with visual or auditory perception and with visual-motor coordination. As they grow older, the problems of attention, organization, social perception, anxiety, and motivation become pre-eminent. In any given developmental college course, many of the learning disabled appear at first glance to be no less able than other students in the class to meet course requirements. However, significant distinctions quickly emerge, and the instructor soon perceives that their academic work varies far more in quality than that of the general developmental student population. Likewise, their daily cognitive and social behavior is often more erratic and unpredictable than that of their peers.

Some illustrations of students with learning disability profiles may prove helpful. James thinks well conceptually and is above average in classroom participation and ability to respond to classroom questions. Yet, he often misses details and tends to have trouble integrating material when reading long selections or writing essays. Frank, a superior student in English, history, and theater arts, does poorly in subjects that use symbolic language, such as mathematics and chemistry. Jane, who performs adequately in classroom discussions, has trouble with tests, particularly when they are timed or when poor spelling is penalized. Eleanor is alert and responsive in class on one day; on another, she seems to have no grasp of the subject matter. Richard, usually a master for remembering details, is frequently unable to synthesize material. He is isolated and often ridiculed by his fellow students.

College programs designed specifically to meet the diverse needs of students who manifest such characteristics have been few and far between. In recent years, however, several programmatic approaches have been implemented across the nation. They include the fully developed, comprehensive model, as well as ancillary programs of support that provide a full- or part-time specialist in learning disabilities within the framework of a learning center. Some approaches involve an admissions and special program combination in order to accommodate learning-disabled students. On occasion, colleges and universities have sponsored case-by-case assistance for students in this category. Time Out to Enjoy, a national organization of and for learning-disabled adults, has recently compiled a guide that classifies college programs according to these different approaches (Ridenour and Johnston, 1981).

The Learning Center Response: A Program Model

In order to reverse the learning-disabled college student's sense of despair and helplessness, teaching strategies should be devised that address each student's abilities, deficiencies, and learning style. The typical learning center that serves a general student population can be very effective in helping this particular student group. However, the process of adapting and operating learning center services for learning-disabled students will require staff members who have academic or professional training in the field of learning disability. Aside from this absolute necessity, it is impossible to prescribe the exact type of support services that are appropriate for learning centers in general, because they differ too widely in structure and in services provided for any one approach to be useful. Nevertheless, it may still prove instructive to outline a model center whose operations can be used as guidelines for typical learning center situations, in which learning-disabled students constitute only a small percentage of the total student users.

The Learning Opportunities Center at Kingsborough Community College in Brooklyn, New York, was the first federally funded comprehensive program for learning-disabled community college students. Its approach has been holistic, and federal support has enabled the Center to provide a total learning environment for students with learning disabilities. It operates through a variety of modes: teaching, tutoring, the development of bypass techniques and coping strategies, a career opportunities course, counseling, and environmental manipulation. Although the service delivery models developed by the Center are comprehensive, they can be adapted to settings in which the learning-disabled student is mixed in with the general learning center student population.

A Learning Center Course. Kingsborough Community College offers courses in developmental reading and English composition to students who fail to achieve minimum levels of competence on its placement examination. From the curricula used in these courses, the Learning Opportunities Center created a combined reading and writing course adapted to the needs of its student clientele. The principal restructuring involved combining reading and writing into a single course that met the pacing needs of these students and worked to overcome their learning deficits as well.

Course goals include analyzing and critically reviewing the written and oral presentations of authors and speakers, organizing and integrating information from different sources, and synthesizing ideas, information, and materials for use in the preparation of written compositions. Lesson units are presented in systematic steps to help students to develop an ability to spot structure, organization, and pattern, which acts to enhance their skills in analyzing material and information. Constantly, the instructor searches for methods and materials that help to achieve these goals. Thus, while this course teaches skills and employs techniques that can be used in any developmental reading and writing course, the emphasis has been placed on motivation, task analysis, and individualization of instruction.

Learning-disabled students need constant encouragement to become active learners. They must be able to analyze, integrate, infer, and challenge. To this purpose, the reading and writing course developed by the Learning Opportunities Center is structured to give students maximum exposure to the use of questioning strategies. They are urged to question what they are told in class, what they hear on television and at home, and what they understand from their own reading. They are required to formulate questions and rephrase ideas prior to, during, and after each learning activity. Projects that foster this active learning process include brief listening work periods, before which students are instructed to listen for the topic or major thought and then to formulate questions about what they hear. Classroom assignments require students to read short passages and prepare questions for someone who has read the same selection.

Students' reading levels are positively affected through implementation of certain principles of memory improvement: organization, association, visualization, and feedback. That is, they are shown how to organize what they have learned into categories, to make associations between items, and to generate visual images. Another objective of the course work is to have learning-disabled students develop proofreading skills. One strategy that has proved particularly effective requires one student to read passages aloud to another student, who questions the clarity of each thought expressed. Another strategy requires the student to read his composition aloud, in reverse order, sentence by sentence, so as to pick up spelling errors. A third technique, which can be utilized both in the classroom and in tutorial sessions, uses current newspaper and magazine articles as models of well-organized writing and as stimuli and sources of ideas for students' expository writing efforts. This adds relevance to the course while allowing students to focus on idiomatic and figurative language useage.

Many problems arise when learning-disabled students are taught in a homogeneous classroom environment. They generally have little faith in their knowledge and in their ability to use the English language. As a result, their written and oral expressions are considerably restricted, and classroom participation and liveliness suffer. Free writing exercises help to make them more at ease with language expression. Brainstorming ideas in small groups, followed by structured questioning, helps these students to organize and recall ideas and information that they may wish to write about. Other strategies that can be employed with these students in a reading and writing classroom or tutorial situation necessitate the isolation of a few critical skills and their constant reinforcement in application to course work materials. Students should be shown how to attack and confront each skill from as many angles as possible. Finally, experience has shown that when classes are small and instruction is individualized, classes divided equally between learning-disabled and general development college students are the most effective in promoting class participation, teacher morale, and student skills growth.

Developing Study Skills and Providing Career Counseling. In addition to working on general language skills and facility, the Learning Opportunities Center has helped learning-disabled students to adjust to college and its academic demands through an intensive orientation and study skills course. This course focuses on general adjustment problems that are particularly worrisome for the learning-disabled student—problems related to the change in environment, to organization of thought, and to management of stress. Topics covered in this course include college life, its rules and opportunities, study skills, time management, student-faculty relations, and test anxiety.

A career development course complements the more academically oriented courses in language and study skills. Here, decision-making and self-monitoring techniques are taught. Students are also helped to explore alternatives to inappropriate career decisions. *Guided Design,* a teaching tool that guides the student in the decision-making process and offers career information and a step-by-step procedure for interpreting this information, is the principal instructional material used in the course. Role playing has proved to be a helpful classroom activity, as have the videotaping of mock interviews, instruction in transactional analysis techniques, and exploration of realistic job options.

Tutoring. Individual tutoring, which is offered to all learning-disabled students for two hours weekly, combines developmental and compensatory techniques that are geared to the students' level of functioning, ability, and goals. Peer tutors staff this service. The Learning Opportunities Center provides several hours of orientation and training to give tutors background in the special needs of learning-disabled students. After this introduction, tutors begin their work, but their training continues. They are under the day-to-day supervision of a learning disabilities specialist, who periodically offers small-group training workshops for peer tutors who are already working. While this model has limitations, it also has significant strengths. Foremost, it engages the interest and increases the understanding of the college community in both the program and the students that it serves. Also, the peer tutors model appropriate student behavior for the learning-disabled students whom they tutor.

Assistance in the basic skills is provided by breaking tasks down into their component subskills, by determining a student's proficiency in each, and by concentrating on the areas of deficiency. In addition to mastering the basic skills, each student is encouraged to become an active participant in establishing goals and evaluating progress. Compensatory and bypass techniques are utilized whenever appropriate. For example, several students have been trained to use taped textbooks and to record selected classroom assignments on tape. Direct training in the use of these techniques and in their application to various courses is very important.

One particular problem for learning-disabled students is their inability to generalize skills to all their course work. Learning Opportunities Center tutors are aware of this difficulty and try to help their students to analyze how they use the skills in question, and they encourage students to transfer these skills consciously from one course to another. Periodically, this process is reviewed, and the students' application of what they have learned is monitored. Tutors also help students to cope with academic demands and develop independence through the use of self-monitoring strategies. Checklists, proofreading techniques, and other aids to enhance this self-monitoring process help students to use acquired skills, function independently, reduce impulsiveness, and cope with frustration.

Counseling. The affective needs of learning-disabled students must also be met if they are to perform effectively in college. Repeated experience of academic and social failure has made many of them profoundly doubtful of their ability and reluctant to function autonomously. A multidimensional counseling program that addresses problems of identity and self-esteem in a variety of ways has been developed by the Learning Opportunities Center to deal with this area of student need. Counseling enables students to improve on their decision-making skills, to ventilate their feelings of isolation, and to modify inflexible styles of functioning. Almost all students find that counseling affords them an opportunity to explore several different problems at the same time, although the initial focus may have been on a single difficult situation—decision making, loneliness, or, possibly, a personal crisis.

One innovative adjunct to the individual and group counseling sessions for project students involves an outreach, cross-age peer tutoring program conducted at the Psychoeducational Clinic of Long Island Hospital in downtown Brooklyn. Here, Learning Opportunities Center students have a chance to tutor younger learning-disabled students. At the same time, they are encouraged to identify and work through feelings associated with the repeated failures that they experienced as children. They become better able to recognize their own abilities through their successful interactions with younger learning-disabled children.

Especially important for counseling support services are constant feedback from peers and opportunities to monitor personal interactions with others. Both have been supplied through a social interaction group, where structured experiences enable students to become more self-aware and to develop social skills. Interactions with family members are another integral part of the counseling process. During family counseling sessions, students and parents are encouraged to share their thoughts and feelings about each other. Frequently, parental concerns are different from student needs. During these sessions, differences are aired, and other problem areas, such as unrealistic parental expectations and lack of structure in the home, are explored.

In summation, the multimodal and varied counseling process offers students a sounding board for their perceptions, ideas, and feelings. It creates an opportunity for them to explore and understand themselves and their interactions with others. Project students can grow within the counseling relationship. The value and effectiveness of this program, however, is not in its focus on the learning disabled as such but rather in its emphasis on responding to individual needs. This counseling approach can also be used with underprepared students, who also suffer from frustration, isolation, failure, and poor self-image.

Becoming an Independent Learner. The development of a healthy self-concept does not need to be confined to a formal counseling situation. The Learning Opportunities Center has attempted, in effect, to establish conditions under which students can function independently. It offers these learning-disabled young adults an opportunity to discover and use their strengths, to see themselves as capable and separate human beings, and to take a positive perspective of their academic and personal futures. This goal of independent functioning has been embedded in all aspects of the Kingsborough Community College program.

In attempting to achieve this objective, project staff members offer optimal rather than maximal support to students in classroom situations.

For each student and for each course subject, a professional counselor makes an early assessment of the degree of intervention needed. Decisions are made jointly between student and counselor. When the student opts for no initial intervention, that decision is respected. Whatever the decision, Learning Opportunities Center staff members continuously monitor the academic progress of all program students.

From the very start of the semester, these students are encouraged to develop effective, independent decision-making skills. The sense of damage and incompetence that many feel tends to diminish as they learn how and when to ask for special help. This help can come in the form of extended time limits for tests and assignments, individually administered tests, and use of tape recorders in class. As students improve their ability to function independently, the degree and number of supports and interventions are gradually reduced.

An example of this process may prove instructive. In the case of one severely disabled, highly distractable, and anxious learning-disabled student, a staff member felt that it was necessary to confer with the student's instructors about possible manifestations of the learning disability in classroom behavior, written work, and test taking. At this point, the student was not a participant in the discussons. Later, the staff member role played a conference situation with the student several times and then accompanied the student to an appointment with one of his instructors. At this time, the student was expected to maintain responsibility for discussion of his problem and to make any requests for special assistance. Gradually, as the result of this type of intervention, the student became able to meet instructors independently.

As noted earlier in this chapter, a lack of good self-monitoring skills and of a developed sense of social awareness prevents many learning-disabled students from accurately assessing their performance in social groups or in conferences with instructors. Certain intervention strategies employed at the Learning Opportunities Center have proved effective in assisting program students with these problems. Role playing and discussions of videotaped mock and in vivo interviews have improved students' ability to interact in college and social situations. Students have also benefited from their participation in preparation of training tapes. These tapes have been of great help not only to those who took part in their preparation but to the general body of program students as well. One taped role played interview in which a student explained his disability to an instructor has proved extremely helpful. This tape is in continuous use as counselors attempt to improve students' effectiveness in their personal contacts with instructors.

It should be remembered that certain academic tasks will always remain difficult, if not impossible, unless bypass procedures are used in a systematic way and on a campuswide basis. During the final examination period, for instance, Kingsborough administrators and faculty have agreed to allow program students to have their examinations administered individually at the Learning Oportunities Center. When necessary, students are able to use individually prepared cue cards during tests and on assignments. These cards help them to implement their test-taking, language, and recall skills and remind them of compensatory or bypass strategies that they will need for the particular occasion. As a case in point, one student was permitted to use a card listing the steps that he needed to follow in writing an essay. In this way, he was prevented from lapsing into the repetitive, rambling style that had characterized his previous essay. The ultimate goal in all these cases of intervention is to reduce participation by staff members during examinations and to develop greater independence in students for the future.

Finally, in addition to the self-monitoring and social awareness skills that can be fostered through judicious counseling by specialists, learning-disabled students need an understanding and responsive college environment that affords them a few special procedures that will help them to avoid occasions of severe stress, tension, and frustration. One example of these special procedures is the semester registration process for project students. This is a difficult time for most college students, but it is particularly stressful for the learning-disabled. Often, they are inflexible and unable to function when instructions are complex or unclear, and they respond poorly in pressured, structured large-group activities. At Kingsborough, through the cooperation of administrators, faculty, and counselors, special registration arrangements have been set up for program students. However, all procedures are presented in such a way as to prevent students from feeling that they are incapable of functioning on their own. In all preregistration conferences, Learning Opportunities Center staff members discuss students' projected course options in a manner calculated to improve their decision-making skills.

Conclusion

Perhaps the most significant contribution of the Learning Opportunities Center has been its impact on faculty members and on general college policy. Through consultaton with Center staff members, Kingsborough Community College faculty have become more aware of the need for individualizing instruction, teaching to the needs, levels, and strengths of all students, extending time limits on tests for some students, and allowing others to use a tape recorder in class. In case conferences, they have been encouraged to share their perceptions of "problem" students.

Many of their initial suspicions and prejudices about learning-disabled students have been modified, if not eliminated altogether. The college administration also has a heightened awareness of the need for flexibility in programming, and it is providing more clearly drawn instructions and guidelines concerning registration procedures, course withdrawal conditions, and minimum credit requirements.

Through its many interactions and interventions with project students and the college community as a whole, the Learning Opportunity Center offers a varied, highly individualized program designed to compensate for and overcome specific learning deficits. In many respects, most underprepared students could benefit from some of the strategies and techniques used for the learning-disabled student. They, too, have difficulty maneuvering in the college environment. They, too, have many negative attitudes and feelings about themselves, as well as authority figures, peers, tests, and learning in general. These students, however, do not need individually administered tests or special registration arrangements, nor do they always require the kind of individual interventions that are routine at the Center. Nevertheless, they could benefit from the seminars on decision-making and test-taking skills that the Center extends to its learning-disabled students. In essence, the Learning Opportunities Center has developed a model for college survival that is helpful not only to learning-disabled students but to underprepared students in general. This holistic approach to education helps students to integrate their varied abilities, interests, and aspirations in a way that also encourages them to function effectively and independently in the academic and social climate of the college community.

References

Hiroto, D. S., and Seligman, M. E. "Generality of Learned Helplessness in Man." *Journal of Personality and Social Psychology*, 1975, *31*, 311–327.
Ridenour, D. M., and Johnston, J. *A Guide to Postsecondary Educational Opportunities for the Learning Disabled*. Oak Park, Ill.: Time Out to Enjoy, 1981.

Irwin Rosenthal was responsible for establishing the Learning Opportunities Center at Kingsborough Community College in Brooklyn, New York, and he has directed the Center since its inception in 1978. This program for learning-disabled students has received wide acclaim and recognition in the press, in scholarly journals and reviews, and in monographic works.

Elaine Fine was a learning specialist at the Center.

Robert de Vight was a learning specialist at the Center. Previously, he was assistant director of the Reading Institute at New York University.

The references included in this chapter are intended for learning center personnel who have little or no formal training in the field of learning disabilities and who wish to understand and assist students who have this handicap.

The Learning-Disabled College Student: Reference Notes

Elaine Caputo-Ferrara

Much of the attention currently being devoted in educational circles to the problem of learning disability is focused on children and teenagers in primary and secondary schools. Learning-disabled college students have not been studied with the same intensity, although interest in their academic welfare has increased markedly in recent years, particularly after passage of the Rehabilitation Act of 1973. The materials described in this section are intended for learning center personnel who have little or no formal training in the field of learning disabilities and who wish to understand and assist students afflicted with this handicap. Since there is little that deals directly with the adult college-level student, resources have been included that are more appropriate for secondary school student populations. However, if used judiciously, they can be helpful and informative with college students as well.

Because the field of college-level learning disabilities is new and ever-changing, learning center personnel need to be aware of current developments in the field, and they should share this information as widely as possible on campus. This sharing can be promoted by a con-

L. Wilson (Ed.). *New Directions for College Learning Assistance: Helping Special Student Groups*, no. 7. San Francisco: Jossey-Bass, March 1982.

scious effort by learning center staff to build up a collection of books, articles, and other printed materials on learning-disabled college students.

Books and Pamphlets

American Council on Education. *Higher Education and the Handicapped 1981 Resource Directory.* Washington, D.C.: American Council on Education, 1981 (designed to help colleges and universities to implement programs providing equal access to postsecondary education).

Brown, D. *Steps to Independence for People with Learning Disabilities.* Washington, D.C.: Closer Look, 1980 (pamphlet written for learning-disabled people, their parents, and professionals in the field).

College Entrance Examination Board. *College Board Admissions Testing Programs for Handicapped Students.* Princeton, N.J.: College Entrance Examination Board, n.d. (a booklet that gives information to handicapped students who wish to take college admissions tests).

Smith, L. *The College Student with a Disability: A Faculty Handbook.* Washington, D.C.: U.S. Government Printing Office, 1980.

Newsletters and Journals

Academic Therapy. Published five times a year, this journal for parents, teachers, and specialists covers reading, learning, and communication disabilities and methods of identification, diagnosis, and remediation. Address: 20 Commercial Boulevard, Novato, Calif, 94947.

Bulletin of the Orton Society. This international publication is issued once a year by the Orton Society, a nonprofit scientific and educational organization for the study and treatment of individuals with dyslexia. Address: 724 York Road, Baltimore, Md. 21204.

Journal of Reading. Published eight times a year, this journal intended for secondary school teachers sometimes prints articles concerning motivational techniques for use with older poor readers. Address: International Reading Association, 800 Barksdale Road, Newark, Del. 19711.

Reading Research Quarterly. This journal describes current research in reading disability and is published four times a year. Address: International Reading Association, 800 Barksdale Road, Newark, Del. 19711.

Teaching Exceptional Children. Published four times a year, this journal is intended for the special education teacher in the primary and secondary school. Address: Council for Exceptional Children, 1920 Association Drive, Reston, Va. 22091.

The Journal of Learning Disabilities. Published ten times a year, this journal emphasizes a multidisciplinary approach to the diagnosis and treatment of learning disabilities. Address: 101 East Ontario Street, Chicago, Ill. 60611.

The LD Observer. This newsletter is published by the Specific Learning Development Association. Address: P.O. Box 237, Wellesley Hills, Mass. 02181.

Publications Available Through the
ERIC Document Reproduction Services

Address: Eric Clearinghouse on Reading and Communications Skills, National Council of Teachers of English, 1111 Kenyon Road, Urbana, Ill. 61801.

Bingham, G., and others. *Working with Adult Exceptional Learners. A Handbook of Suggestions for Assessment, Educational Planning, and Instructional Strategies,* 1978 (ED 167 725).

Christ, F. (Ed.). *College Reading Goals for the 70s: Proceedings of the Annual Conference of the Western College Reading Association,* 1970 (ED 166 677).

Loxterman, A. *College Composition and the Invisible Handicap,* 1978 (ED 168 016).

Mosby, R. J., and Tharpe, K. *Understanding Secondary Learning-Disabled Students: A Developmental Bypass Approach,* 1977 (ED 162 447).

Rehmann, S. *Piagetian Cognitive Levels of Adult Basic Educational Students Related to Teaching Methods and Materials,* 1979 (ED 167 829).

Richards, A. *Writing Dysfunction: A Problem in College Composition Courses,* 1977 (ED 158 271).

Rogan, L., and Hartman, L. *A Follow-Up Study of Learning-Disabled Children as Adults,* 1976 (ED 163 728).

Materials on Existing Programs

The following materials sample existing programs and facilities for the learning-disabled person who is interested in postsecondary education.

"Colleges/Universities That Accept Students with Learning Disabilities." A list prepared by the Association for Children with Learning Disabilities. Address: 4156 Library Road, Pittsburgh, Pa. 15324.

Directory of Educational Facilities for the Learning Disabled. Address: Academic Therapy Publications, 20 Commercial Boulevard, Novato, Calif. 94947.

Fact Sheet: The Learning-Disabled Adult and Postsecondary Education. Information on a sampling of postsecondary institutions with LD programs. Address: Closer Look Resource Center, P.O. Box 1492, Washington, D.C. 20013.

Fielding, P. M. (Ed.). *A National Directory of Four-Year Colleges, Two-Year Colleges, and Post–High School Training Programs for Young People with Learning Disabilities.* Tulsa, Okla.: Partners in Publishing, 1975.

Kranes, J. E. *The Hidden Handicap.* New York: Simon and Schuster, 1980. The appendix includes a section entitled "United States Learning Disability Centers for Young Adults Ages Eighteen and Above."

Osman, B. B. *Learning Disabilities: A Family Affair.* New York: Random House, 1979. One appendix includes a section entitled "Colleges, Universities, and Postsecondary School Programs."

Associations

American Council on Education, One Dupont Circle, Washington, D.C. 20026.

Association of Learning-Disabled Adults, P.O. Box 9722, Washington, D.C. 20016.

Closer Look: National Information Center for the Handicapped, P.O. Box 1492, Washington, D.C. 20013.

Independent Educational Counselors Association, 128 Great Road, Bedford, Mass. 01730.

International Reading Association, 800 Barksdale Road, Newark, Del. 19711.

LD Adult Committee/Association for Children with Learning Disabilities, 4156 Library Road, Pittsburgh, Pa. 15234.

National Council of Teachers of English, 1111 Kenyon Road, Urbana, Ill. 61801.

National Education Association, 1201 Sixteenth St., N.W., Washington, D.C. 20036.

National Network of Learning-Disabled Adults, P.O. Box 3130, Richardson, Tex. 75080.

Orton Dyslexia Society, 8415 Bellona Lane, Towson, Md. 21204.

Elaine Caputo-Ferrara is associate director of the Office of Special Academic Services at the Brooklyn Center of Long Island University. She directs a developmental reading program and an academic and counseling program for students who are deficient in the basic skills.

*The distinct advantage of the learning center in ESL
instruction lies in its particular capacity to deal with
each student's individual needs.*

Assisting English-as-a-Second-Language Students

John Klosek

If the 1970s have become known as the decade in which large numbers of underprepared students flocked to college and university campuses, the 1980s may very well become the decade of the English-as-a-second-language (ESL) student. Although the number of ESL students will not approach that of the underprepared students who entered college in the 1970s, ESL students will be increasingly sought after as enrollments continue to decline, and they will become a very recognizable new student group, adding to the heterogeneity that is so characteristic of today's institutions of higher learning.

Since the mid seventies, the foreign student population in the United States has been growing at a rate ranging between 12 percent and 16 percent a year. In 1978–1979, it stood at well over a quarter million students. In many institutions, foreign students already represent between 10 percent and 20 percent of the total enrollment (Boyan and Julian, 1980). Immigration is another source of students whose native language is not English. In many big city public schools, speakers of other languages constitute as much as 30 percent of the student body. In a few years, these students will be ready to enter college.

Increased immigration and the prestige that American degrees have abroad will provide an abundant supply of students whose native lan-

L. Wilson (Ed.). *New Directions for College Learning Assistance:
Helping Special Student Groups*, no. 7. San Francisco: Jossey-Bass, March 1982.

guage is not English. ESL enrollments will be considerably augmented by a large influx of students for whom English is, at best, a second language, and who have been attracted to postsecondary education by open-admissions policies and academic support programs. Thus, individual ESL students will vary tremendously in academic preparation and in English language background. It is imperative for those who must deal with this distinct group of nontraditional students to keep in mind that their needs are not the same as those of other such groups and that the instructional methods that work with one group will not necessarily work with another. The label *ESL* should only be used at the generic level; it should not be used to channel such students into a predetermined curriculum of course offerings.

Most of the prestigious universities in the United States have had intensive English courses for speakers of other languages for some time. In the aftermath of the Second World War, these programs were directed at the elite foreign visiting student. Local immigrant populations were consistently ignored. Tuition costs, academic demands, and rigid entrance requirements put such programs far beyond the reach of most nonnative English speakers residing in the United States. ESL programs were rare indeed on standard American campuses. Now, with the changing international situation, the energy crisis, open enrollment, and a host of new social and economic factors, American education has become more accessible. At the same time, the pool of potential ESL students has expanded markedly.

Prior to open admission, many resident immigrants were barred from college by low Scholastic Aptitude Test (SAT) scores and low high school grade point averages. As college doors began to open in the early 1970s and as the pool of available students began to shrink in the late 1970s, colleges and universities became more interested in addressing the needs of the non-English-speaking student who was academically underprepared for college work. English language institutes around the country continue to prepare visiting foreign students for study in the United States. Now, as domestic enrollments shrink, many postsecondary institutions have lowered their English language entrance requirements for both immigrant and foreign students. This means that students who, in the past, would have been required to master the English language before they began full-time college study are now being admitted to freshman composition courses for which they are not prepared and that they cannot pass.

ESL Student Profiles

Foreign students generally fall into two categories—those who have been educated in their native language and those for whom English was the medium of instruction. Students in the latter category sometimes find themselves placed in ESL classes, in many cases for the wrong reason, because they were educated abroad. Some may need special courses; others may not. Serious problems arise when foreign students for whom English is a native language are put in ESL classes. They more properly belong in regular remedial courses, since what they are learning is not a second language but a second dialect. Placing such people in standard ESL classes invariably results in a lot of resentment and very little learning.

Generally speaking, foreign-educated students, both those who were educated in their native language and those for whom English was the language of instruction, have good study skills and know how to organize their ideas in an orderly fashion. The most likely explanation is that these are the best students, who were handpicked for study abroad. That explanation would also account for their apparent advantage over the average American student. However, they probably are not representative of the entire population from which they come. An interesting observation about foreign-educated students is that on standardized achievement tests, such as the California Achievement Test, they usually score two to four grade levels higher on comprehension than on vocabulary, while native English speaking students generally exhibit the opposite pattern (Podrid, 1980). This would appear to be an inexplicable anomaly, for how can one understand a passage without knowing the vocabulary? One possible explanation is that good reading skills—that is, the ability to make inferences, locate main ideas, find details, and make judgments from contextual clues—enable foreign-educated students to answer comprehension questions with a reasonable degree of accuracy. However, vocabulary tests, where words are presented either in isolation or in short phrases, do not provide the contextual clues that enable them to use their reading skills to determine meaning.

In addition to poor vocabulary, foreign-educated students frequently have difficulty mastering the fine points of English grammar, such as tense and aspectual systems, articles, prepositions, word order, and count and mass nouns, to name only a few. Idiomatic usage creates difficulty for such students, who often present the literal translation from their native language, frequently with unintended humorous effect.

One area in which English-medium foreign students differ from other foreign students is fluency. Years of exposure to and use of English results in a facility of expression, although that expression is not always grammatical or idiomatic. Students who have been educated by British-trained teachers sometimes beguile their American professors with British accents. These students are apt to "speak better English" than many of the professors. It frequently comes as a surprise to their professors when such students prove to have no more than an eighth-grade vocabulary level and a tenth-grade reading comprehension level. Also, they make an average of two grammatical or idiomatic errors per sentence. They are able to make the initial excellent impression by relying on a few stereotyped expressions and by avoiding areas of potential difficulty.

The third group of ESL students—the most difficult to characterize —is composed of American-educated immigrants. This group includes recent immigrants as well as American-born individuals whose home language is not English. Sometimes, these students have excellent preparation; other times, they need remediation in every area. The latter group is particularly enigmatic. These students are commonly referred to as remedial or urban ESL students. More often than not, they live in communities where their native language is the principal means of communication, members of their group predominate in the schools that they attend, and most of their business and social contacts are with people who speak their language. Understandably, after attending English-speaking schools and living within a superordinate English-speaking society, they do develop an ability to communicate. Yet, their speech patterns can scarcely be called standard English. Rather, they have many of the characteristics ascribed to the pidgin languages (Schumann, 1978). Unlike foreign-educated students, their vocabulary may be superior to their reading comprehension level, in which they resemble the prototype of the American remedial student (Byrd and Klosek, 1979). They may also lack study skills and motivation, like underprepared students. However, in contrast to the student who is only deficient in academic skills, the American-educated immigrant student will have many problems with grammar and idiomatic expressions, and, in these instances, he will again resemble students in the foreign-educated group. Thus, the urban ESL student is a hybrid, who requires both the intensive language instruction that foreign students receive and the personal counseling and study skills development that are made available to underprepared students.

ESL Students and Learning Center Services

These three kinds of ESL students, who have different needs and proficiency levels, are often found in the same class. In many institutions, because of financial constraints, long-standing traditions, and, in some cases, xenophobic attitudes, little can be done to alter existing course structures and curricula. College and university learning centers, because of their intrinsic flexibility, can adapt to the needs of the diverse ESL student groups and provide what amounts to individualized instruction that is geared to each student's particular needs. The learning center is especially helpful on campuses that lack extensive language institutes: Here, the services offered can usually be classified into three main categories: reading and writing laboratories, individualized tutoring, and small-group workshops. Originally designed for the needs of underprepared English-speaking students, these services can easily be adapted to fit the purposes of ESL students.

Language Skills Laboratories. The reading laboratory, which is usually offered in conjunction with developmental reading courses, is designed to give students additional practice in developing comprehension skills. Students are given a diagnostic reading test, and test results become the basis of an individualized program of study. Students' progress, as measured by periodic reassessments, leads to modifications in their programs. The distinct advantage of this kind of instruction is that students receive immediate feedback that tells them what they are doing right and where they are making errors.

For the ESL student, regardless of the level of academic preparation and English language skills, the reading laboratory serves to provide additional practice in the development of reading comprehension skills and vocabulary enlargement. As already noted, underprepared ESL students are weakest in comprehension. In their case, the laboratory can be used to reinforce such reading skills as making inferences, locating details, and making judgments. For the foreign-educated student, the reading laboratory will put vocabulary expansion at the top of the list of priorities. Many reading development series in the regular curriculum can be adapted by appending vocabulary exercises that give the ESL student an opportunity to discuss what he has read and to ask questions about it. Here, the object is not to learn how to read but to learn how to read faster, to acquire English rhetorical styles, recognize cultural nuances, and, most importantly, acquire a college-level vocabulary.

Reading texts especially designed for ESL students eliminate the need for improvisation. *Reader's Choice* (Baudoin and others, 1977) and *Reading English for Academic Study* (Long and others, 1980) are excellent resource materials. Each unit addresses a specific reading skill, such as skimming, guessing vocabulary from context, and using semantic relationships, and each unit is followed by a reading passage, an array of comprehension questions, and a variety of word study and grammar exercises. The lab instructor can determine which exercises will have the most ameliorative effect on the student's reading skills. Also, every reading laboratory should have dictionaries useful to students who have only a minimal English vocabulary. The best to my knowledge is *Longman Dictionary of Contemporary English.* Each entry includes several examples of standard usage, and entries are not cluttered with potentially confusing etymological explanations and arcane and obsolete definitions.

Writing laboratories, like their reading counterparts, are a required component of developmental writing courses at many colleges and universities. Underprepared non-ESL students frequently have difficulty with writing assignments because they speak a nonstandard dialect. Another source of difficulty stems from the use of informal conversational style in writing. The typical individualized writing laboratory approach for this group of students involves the diagnostic-prescriptive method, in which students are asked to work on such problem areas as sentence fragments, split infinitives, subject-verb agreement, and coherence and organization.

Underprepared ESL students need to develop the same skills, but they also have special problems with English usage, notably with articles, prepositions, modifiers, and auxiliaries. As a rule, foreign-educated students try to limit their written work to simple declarative sentences. What they have to do, even at advanced levels, is to develop a variety of writing styles. This can be done through sentence-combining and -rewriting exercises, both of which focus on the inflectional, coordinative, and subordinative aspects of language. The ESL laboratory should aim to produce error-free writing that will allow students to concentrate on the varieties of style.

As in the reading laboratory, instructors can adapt materials from standard English composition texts and grammar reviews. Exercises and drills can also be developed by learning center staff members under the guidance and supervision of ESL instructors. Indeed, consistent attention over a few years to the creation of resource materials will lead to an inexpensive, yet imaginative and effective, laboratory library. Suggested texts for ESL students' personal use include *Mastering American English* (Taylor, 1956), an old standby containing numerous exercises on major grammatical points that is particularly useful for individualized work. *Write Away* (Gallingane and Byrd, 1977, 1979) provides sentence-rewriting and sentence-combining exercises, with each unit focused on a single grammatical point. COMP (Alexander and Cornelius, 1978) combines reading with writing practice. Such materials are admirably suited to individualized practice in the writing laboratory.

In addition to the reading laboratory and writing laboratory, most institutions have—and if not, they should seriously consider establishing—a foreign-language laboratory. This can be a very effective tool in assisting ESL students to speak and pronounce correctly, and it can easily be integrated into standard learning center activities. Once ESL teachers are acquainted with the laboratory's potential and are given a detailed referral system, the lab can become an efficient and cost-effective means for individualizing instruction. Students should be scheduled to attend the lab once or twice a week to follow up on their classroom activities. Here, too, the diagnostic-prescriptive methodology must be utilized if the students are to receive individualized attention.

Many fine commercially prepared packages are available for use in the language laboratory. *Pronunciation Drills* (Trager and Henderson, 1956) and *Stress and Intonation* (English Language Services, Inc., 1967) are excellent when used in conjunction with an ESL speech course. For individual grammar practice, two sets of tapes can be recommended: *Oral Pattern Drills* (Dixon, 1963) and *Progressive Audio-Lingual Drills* (Steiglitz, 1970). Unfortunately, in-house materials are technically difficult to develop because of the extraordinary amount of time required to write, rehearse, record, and test new language laboratory materials. In consequence, learning centers should try to purchase materials tailored to their means and to their students' needs.

A word of caution is appropriate at this point. The language laboratory should not be viewed as a panacea for all ills, as it was in the fifties and early sixties. However, it does have a place in the total ESL language program. It can be compared to the gym in which the athlete develops the physical fitness that he needs in order to excel in his particular sporting event. At first glance, lifting weights may appear to have little to do with football or swimming, but athletes use weight training to build strength and enhance their chances of winning. Similarly, language laboratory activities—repetition and grammatical substitution drills, for example—may seem to have little to do with communication or composition. Yet, in the long run, these repetitive exercises are just what is necessary to perfect an ESL student's grammar usage and, ultimately, to make him a more effective communicator and writer.

Tutoring Assistance. The learning center is often the primary source of tutoring assistance on the college or university campus. In almost all cases, peer tutoring is offered in a variety of subject areas, including English. While tutoring typically is used to provide individualized help in areas of student weakness, this service adjunct of the learning center can also be reoriented to afford ESL students the type of language practice that they cannot get outside an academic setting. It may seem strange, but ESL students frequently complain that they do not have opportunities to engage in meaningful, sustained conversations with Americans. Peer tutoring can help to fill this void. Students should be encouraged to visit the learning center laboratory, not in order to work on any specific problem in grammar or writing but in order to spend an hour in conversation with a tutor. In these sessions, students could easily discuss course requirements, the grading system, the curriculum, and college procedures, rules, and regulations. Individually, conversation practice at this level is far more effective than classroom discussions. Most students are less inhibited and more willing to take risks in individualized situations. Moreover, correction does not entail a loss of face or respect, as it can in a classroom situation; this is important for some language groups.

Most learning centers are aware of the need to provide some training or orientation for tutors. In the case of the ESL tutor, it is often falsely assumed that anyone who speaks a language can also teach it. This could not be further from the truth. It is true neither of teachers nor tutors. There is a vast difference between knowing how to speak a language and knowing how to teach it. To be of assistance to others in learning English, tutors and teachers alike need a thorough understanding of English grammar, a familiarity with the psychology of learning, a knowledge of ESL teaching methods, and a sympathetic attitude towards ESL students. In the case of tutors, it may be impractical to insist on all the preceding; for instructors, exceptions cannot be made. Nevertheless, learning centers should insist that each tutor have a modicum of training, experience, or both in the required areas. Tutor orientation or training sessions should precede all laboratory, workshop, or individualized contact with ESL students.

Walk-in Workshops. Walk-in workshops, like individualized tutoring, are a productive and cost-efficient learning center service for ESL students. In a typical writing workshop for American students, each student arrives with problems that he would like to work on, and an experienced tutor provides explanations and exercises. The tutor may find it useful to group students in distinct problem areas or to teach a particular grammar or writing difficulty in the manner of a seminar. The same methodology is useful for ESL students. In small groups, some of the trust and security of the individualized tutoring session will be lost. However, informality of setting and teaching methods will enable the workshop leader to minimize student reticence.

Conclusion

An important fact to remember with all teaching, but particularly with ESL teaching, is that what is taught is not necessarily what is learned. ESL teachers make a clear distinction between input and intake (Corder, 1974). It seems that, in order to learn a linguistic structure, the student must be in a state of readiness. Here, the second-language student resembles the child who is learning his native language. At one time or another, most of us have probably observed that language correction has little or no effect on the child's language output. If a child says, "Daddy dog," and his mother replies, "Yes, that's daddy's dog; say 'Daddy's dog,'" the child may respond by saying "Daddy dog," with no attention to the possessive ending. The correct input does not become intake because the child is not ready to acquire the structure in question (Taylor, 1976).

Similar phenomena have been observed with ESL students. Unlike children, however, they do not eventually achieve perfect mastery of the language (Selinker, 1974). Yet, we can help to ensure that at least some of the input becomes intake by following a few simple principles. First, we should teach what is appropriate to the proficiency level of the student. Grammatical structures should be graded by difficulty, so that the simple can serve as a foundation for the complex. Second, to acquire true linguistic proficiency, the student needs concerted practice. It has already been noted that learning a rule is not much help in producing the language unless the student has an opportunity to practice, make errors, correct mistakes, and develop fluency and ease in speaking. The major goal of an ESL learning center program should be to develop language skills, not to impart knowledge about the language. Third, the student will remember best the elements that he initiates himself; this means that he should be given the chance to use the language creatively as he tries to communicate his ideas and feelings (LaForge, 1975).

It should be kept in mind that the distinct advantage of the learning center in ESL instruction lies in its particular capacity to deal with students' individual needs. Given the diversity of the ESL student group, the fact that the laboratory setting enables students of different levels of English language proficiency to proceed at their own pace, learning only what they need to learn, solves what would otherwise seem an unsurmountable problem. The reading laboratory can be used to allow ESL students to hone skills in which they are weakest. The writing laboratory can help them to integrate the grammatical and rhetorical points taught in the classroom into their composition. The language laboratory can provide reinforcement in specific areas of grammar and pronunciation. Tutoring and walk-in workshops complement these offerings by giving individualized help on particular problems of concern. They can also be useful in providing ESL students with a setting in which to practice communicating in English. In summary, the learning center should be regarded as a pivotal part of the academic language instruction offered to ESL students on college and university campuses.

References

Alexander, L. G., and Cornelius, E. T. *COMP: Exercises in Comprehension and Composition.* New York: Longman, 1978.

74

Baudoin, E. M., and others. *Readers' Choice: A Reading Skills Textbook for Students of English as a Second Language*. Ann Arbor: University of Michigan Press, 1977.

Boyan, D. R., and Julian, A. C. (Eds.). *Open Doors: 1978–1979—Report on International Educational Exchange*. New York: Institute of International Education, 1980.

Byrd, D., and Klosek, J. "The Urban ESL Student: A Preliminary Report." Paper presented at the 13th annual TESOL convention, Boston, March 1979.

Corder, S. P. "The Significance of Learners' Errors." In J. Richards (Ed.), *Error Analysis: Perspectives on Second Language Acquisition*. New York: Longman, 1974.

Dixon, R. J. *Oral Pattern Drills in Fundamental English*. Text and audio tapes. New York: Regents, 1963.

English Language Services, Inc. *Drills and Exercises in English Pronunciation—Stress and Intonation*. Parts 1 and 2, with texts and audio tapes. New York: Collier-Macmillan, 1967.

Gallingane, G., and Byrd, D. *Write Away: A Course for Writing English as a Second Language*. Books 1 and 2. New York: Collier Macmillan International, 1977, 1979.

LaForge, P. G. *Research Profiles with Community Language Learning*. Apple River, Ill.: Counseling Learning Institute, 1975.

Long, M., and others. *Reading English for Academic Study*. Rowley, Mass.: Newbury House, 1980.

Longman Dictionary of Contemporary English. New York: Longman, 1978.

Podrid, A. "Report on the Reading Laboratory for the Academic Year 1979–80." Unpublished manuscript, Long Island University, 1980.

Schumann, J. *The Pidginization Process: A Model for Second Language Acquisition*. Rowley, Mass.: Newbury House, 1978.

Selinker, L. "InterLanguage." In J. Richards (Ed.), *Error Analysis: Perspectives on Second Language Acquisition*. New York: Longman 1974.

Stieglitz, F. *Progressive Audio-Lingual Drills in English*. New York: Regents, 1970.

Taylor, G. *Mastering American English*. New York: McGraw-Hill, 1956.

Taylor, I. *Introduction to Psycholinguistics*. New York: Holt, Rinehart and Winston, 1976.

Trager, E. C., and Henderson, S. C. *The PD's: Pronunciation Drills for Learners of English*. Text and audio tapes. Encino, Calif.: English Language Services, 1956.

John Klosek is director of the English Language Institute at the Brooklyn Center of Long Island University. He has taught in several ESL and teacher preparation programs since 1975, and his publications have appeared in TESOL Quarterly *and* Cognition.

When a learning center offers students
self-management skills, it is not like giving fish to a
hungry man but rather like teaching the man to
fish for himself.

Self-Management Skills:
A Curriculum for
College Learning Centers

Luis Nieves

As American universities expand their admissions policies to offer higher education to nontraditional and underprepared students, the concept of the college learning center grows in importance. Over half of American colleges are operating learning centers today (Sullivan, 1980). These centers have been developed in response to a new population of students that differs in significant ways from the student body served in the past. Until the 1960s, colleges had little need or incentive to extend educational opportunity to underprepared students, and they knew how to teach highly motivated and academically prepared students. The learning center concept, then, grew out of an emerging need to offer full and equal educational opportunity while maintaining the standards of achievement characteristic of higher education.

Learning centers have generally provided basic skills training and various forms of academic and personal advisory services. The ability of these centers to offer both effective remedial education and relevant advisement grows with each year's experience. It can be anticipated that these two crucial components of the learning center will continue to improve and expand.

L. Wilson (Ed.). *New Directions for College Learning Assistance:*
Helping Special Student Groups, no. 7. San Francisco: Jossey-Bass, March 1982.

However, it is this author's belief that a third major component is needed for the effectiveness of centers to increase. Adding one specific form of self-management skills training to the existing components of basic skills and academic and personal advising can greatly assist under-prepared students in becoming more competent learners. This self-management skills curriculum is an instructional component involving psychological abilities that are related to academic performance.

Definitions

Self-management can be defined as the conscious, deliberate, and effective governance of controllable events, decisions, behaviors, and interactions that affect a person's self-interests. It refers to actions, thoughts, and emotions directed toward maximizing an individual's goals. These self-control activities can be of many different kinds. Some are bound to a particular situation; therefore, they are idiosyncratic or unique. Others are part of a general set of self-management principles. This chapter argues the position that every learning center can be enhanced by effective teaching and demonstration of self-management principles. Chapters in various *New Directions for College Learning Assistance* sourcebooks have cogently outlined a set of components required for a complete and effective center. Garner (1980) argued for a basic skills center and specialized services for needs of atypical students, such as the handicapped. Whyte (1980) convincingly espoused group and individual components to balance the basic skills center. These models and many others have now become generally characteristic of the emerging college learning center concept. Very few authors, however, report a component that systematically offers, teaches, or demonstrates the skills that are fundamental to successful functioning and "studenting."

For example, regardless of their ability scores, race, economic resources, and other characteristics, successful students know and practice some fundamental self-management skills. Success in vocational and personal endeavors is also based on the practice and maintenance of these same psychological or self-management skills. Reviewing the literature on the minority college student, Nieves (1978b) concluded that psychological skills are fundamental to educational skills; indeed, they may even be the foundation on which the acquisition of academic skills is based. If they are, then it would be reasonable, even imperative, to add psychological skills training to the other basic components of the college learning skills center.

When persons working in learning centers are first presented with the concept of adding psychological skills development to their services, they tend to respond that helping individuals to become self-sufficient is already their goal. At first glance, general counseling is seen as the way to develop self-management skills. However, under the definition proposed here, the term *self-management* refers to a method or set of techniques that students can use to increase their ability to succeed in an academic setting. Thus, self-management principles are not a set of abstract goals. They are a set of techniques that are specific, concrete, learnable, and fundamental to the more generalized quality that Bandura (1977) has termed *self-efficacy*—more commonly known as *competence*.

Although it was believed originally that competence was a natural result of innate intelligence, it is now understood as a set of learnable psychological skills. The competent student has somehow acquired these skills and uses them effectively. However, the incompetent student can learn them and, through their application, become a competent student. This simple proposition defines the main idea of this chapter. First, it is assumed that every student who stays in school voluntarily wants to be a competent student. Second, it is assumed that competence can be achieved by applying self-management skills within the student's environmental reality to the tasks and activities of college and university life.

Teaching Self-Management Skills
in a Learning Center: A Model

There are levels of personal efficacy that, if reached, would increase the probability of successful academic performance at any level. It is frequently assumed that personal life skills are the result of a successful educational process. Thus, such skills are rarely taught or assessed within the educational system.

The terms *life skills, coping skills, self-help skills,* and *self-control skills* all refer to the specific set of personality skills or characteristics that are applied to daily and developmental problems in the course of an individual's life experience. This experience spans the unique social, economic, family, and personal realities that make up the individual's environment. Three assumptions underlie the following paragraphs: First, the positive application of self-management skills to life events and subsequently to educational opportunities determines the level of an individual's success or failure. Second, it is possible for an indivdiual to have these life skills but fail to apply them, as the number of people who can demonstrate skill in test situations but cannot apply the same skills in life situations shows. Third, all successful students, as measured by criteria of achievement and satisfaction, apply these basic psychological skills to life events.

The nature of the skills and characteristics needed for success are strongly tied to developmental levels. Consequently, the psychological skills needed by a ten-year-old in the fourth grade are not the same as those needed by a fifteen-year-old in the ninth grade. Another source of variance is the environmental demands on the individual. In general, skills develop faster when environmental demands increase. However, if demands exceed developmental capability, then forms of breakdown results.

A look at the relationship between the special demand characteristics of the environment and the individual's developmental level is important to an understanding of academic achievement. For example, the special demands that a highly competitive academic environment makes on an underprepared student can intensify his or her poor adjustment. It is important first to understand the special requirements of each environment and general experience, then to relate that understanding to the personal or coping skills that the individual needs in order to succeed.

Educators frequently ask what personal and psychological skills are most critical for students' success. Psychologists' answers depend on their particular theoretical persuasions. Nevertheless, most would agree that there are at least five domains of psychological functioning or skills: cognitive, behavioral, affective, biological, and sensory. Two other domains that rarely receive attention but are distinguishably different are the interpersonal and imagery domains. Many professionals view interpersonal functioning as an aspect of the individual's behavior and imagery is seen as an extension of the cognitive domain.

Lazarus (1981) reasons, however, that these two modalities should be included in a definition of psychological skills since they represent identifiably different sets of activities. The question is whether all human functioning is included in the seven modalities. Lazarus (1973) claims that psychology has repeatedly relied on investigations of the seven modalities. If this claim is just, we may infer that a basic text in psychology comprehensively organized around the seven modalities will fully incorporate all available knowledge in psychology.

Thus, search for the personal skills related to academic performance is governed by the seven personality modalities. Some key questions to ask are these: What self-help skills are related to each modality? Which of these skills can be taught? What methods of teaching should be used? For what population? In what settings? Are some skills more important in certain settings than in others?

Although there are no panaceas, we can assume that more effective personal functioning will follow if an individual's personal coping or self-help skills are increased. Can more effective personal functioning be translated into effective academic functioning? To answer this question, we must examine the principles related to self-directed strategies of change in the context of each of the personality modalities and assume that each skill deficit can be associated with one of the seven modalities. The application of this set of generalized skills will permit the development of specific and effective approaches tailored to particular academic efforts.

There is significant evidence that self-regulation is an important ingredient of all types of accomplishment. Athletes regulate effort and concentration (Mahoney, 1979a). Novelists regulate time and pacing. The general principles of all these self-regulating efforts are the same. What varies is the application to an individual's life circumstances and personal style. The latter is unique and rarely fully understood. The general principles, however, are the foundations that produce competence when mixed with personality variables. A brief description of some of these generalized skills as they relate to the seven domains of personality follows.

Behavioral Skills Training. The ABC paradigm of behavior is the fundamental formula for the application of behavior control. *A* refers to the antecedents of behavior. Every act, simple or complex, has one or more antecedents. To manage and direct behavior, we must consciously or subconsciously attend to these antecedents. When a student comments that he or she gets very tired after supper and usually takes a nap, the antecedent to taking a nap (behavior) is having supper (another behavior). Similarly, there are antecedents of study behavior—avoidance of study behavior, concentration, going to the library, and so on. Thus, every behavior that an individual desires to improve can be changed by the manipulation of antecedents. Antecedents can be thoughts, images, sensations, feelings, or interactions of all these. The ability to identify the antecedent of the behavior targeted for change is a coping or self-management skill.

B in the ABC paradigm stands for the behavior itself. What behaviors do we want to increase or decrease? In most learning center contexts, it should be relatively easy to list the behaviors that each student needs to decrease or increase in order to maximize effective academic functioning. These behaviors then become the specific targets for self-management. The self-management skill here is to describe the behavior that the student wants to change and the direction of change desired effectively and simply.

C stands for the consequences of a particular behavior. A behavior that leads to positive results (rewards) or that is associated with some rewarding event will have a higher probability of being repeated than a behavior that leads to negative results. We all manipulate consequences (rewards) for others, or at least we try to. Counselors try to demonstrate the connection between good study behavior and academic success. Application of this understanding to students' life situations can help students to develop the motivation to direct their own behavior.

The understanding and application of behavior principles is the basis for the now famous time management workshops so popular in industry. The application of behavior principles is also the basis on which athletes maintain rigid practice and training schedules. Behavior management skills are the hallmarks of excellence and competence.

Another way to view self-management is to conceive of one's personality as the sum of one's actions, thoughts, feelings, relationships, sense, imagery, and chemistry (Lazarus, 1976). Self-management then becomes the regulation of one's personality resources. Development of positive thinking, controlling negative emotions, developing relationships, enhancing sensory sensitivity, utilizing coping imagery, and maintaining physical health—all these represent self-management outcomes. When the personality is working harmoniously to further academic achievement or career development or to deal with life problems, the result is competence or self-efficacy.

The idea is to teach students to apply principles of behavior modification to study and other academic behaviors. Successful, competent students demonstrate high levels of behaviors that promote academic goals and aspirations and low levels of behaviors that compete with academic goals and aspirations. This balance does not occur by chance. Since most of these students must apply some form of behavioral self-management skills, the implication is that, while behavior can be the target of a self-management exercise, the other personality modalities must also be utilized in complementary and supportive ways.

Cognitive Skills Training. Lazarus (1981), Meichenbaum (1975), and Beck (1976) have enhanced our knowledge about the relationship between thought patterns and complex human functioning. Certain categories of thoughts can promote or interfere with general well-being and goal-directed functioning. All three authors draw on the writings of Epictetus, who said that man is disturbed not by events but by the view that he takes of them.

The views that many underprepared students hold regarding their own functioning, expectations, beliefs, and aspirations have been randomly molded. For example, every person has a particular pattern of self-talk: automatically stated phrases that pass through the mind without challenge. We react to these phrases as truths that cannot be compromised. Irrational self-talk is the foundation for a great deal of human dysfunction (Ellis, 1977).

Irrational self-talk is based on irrational ideas. Addressing the mood problems of minority college students, Nieves (1978a) listed irrational ideas commonly held by these students. These ideas include "I'm not smart enough to be in college," "I'm not the equal of most of the other college students," and "Most of what happens to me is out of my control." These irrational ideas become the foundation for self-talk that disorganize students' efforts to complete assignments. "Oh, what's the use?" rendered planning irrelevant, and "It won't change anything" made effort useless.

Part of the learning center curriculum should include teaching the relationship among external events, students' perception of these events, students' interpretations of these events (irrational ideas and self-talk), and their emotional or physical responses. An understanding of this relationship would then become the foundation for teaching the skills needed to assess and identify irrational ideas. Students should be taught to refute irrational ideas, promote rational thinking, and use rational emotive imagery and other techniques to develop a thinking style that is supportive of academic and other life-related goals.

Researchers and practitioners have developed a rather comprehensive data base on self-management of thinking styles. Psychological therapy programs have developed special applications for symptom relief, and education and industry have found goal enhancement to be a useful and effective approach. Recently, industry has demonstrated a particular interest in teaching psychological skills to executives and other critical personnel. The world of athletics (Mahoney, 1979a) is also teaching athletes how to manage psychological attributes to increase performance.

Interpersonal Skills Training. Assertiveness training is a very well-developed area in the psychological community. Numerous training manuals outline the specific behaviors, thoughts, and interaction skills that comprise the assertive style. One early teacher of assertiveness training (Salter, 1949) recognized the relationship between assertive styles and optimism or general well-being. More relevant to our concern with academic performance, Salter trained individuals in assertive styles as a way of overcoming performance barriers.

Lazarus (1958) was another early proponent of assertiveness training to increase self-efficacy and promote general well-being. More recently, Lazarus and Fay (1975) coauthored a self-help primer on assertiveness training that can easily serve as a curriculum outline. There are many such manuals on the market. Another particularly good one is that by Lange and Jakubowski (1976). These authors point out that all assertiveness training elaborates on four basic themes. The first theme teaches the differences between aggressive, assertive, and polite behavior in interactions with other people and associates these differences with the responses or likely consequences of each behavior. The second theme teaches the thought patterns that support assertive behavioral styles. The third theme teaches individuals the reasonable rights that each of us has and should give to others. The fourth theme elaborates on use of basic communication skills in phrasing and articulating requests, giving information, and so on. Lazarus and Nieves (1980) provide an overview that relates the various assertiveness techniques to each of the personality modalities.

Communication skills are especially valuable in a general self-management program. Knowing how to say what one means directly and simply can avoid complications resulting from misunderstandings. Underprepared students typically show a reticence to make requests, assert their rights, and communicate their thoughts and feelings directly. The communications training manual by Gottman and others (1976) is a valuable corollary to the overall assertiveness training curriculum.

Sensory Control Training. The relationship between sensory states and performance has long been recognized as a key connection and target for self-control. In recent times, relaxation training has become the prime strategy for offsetting the negative effects of anxiety and other intrusive emotions. Both the professional and the lay literature have shown great interest in the control of stress (Woolfolk and Richardson, 1978). The recent interest in Zen and yoga indicates an awareness and application of sensory control. Entire therapies have been designed around maximizing the mind-body connection (Lazarus, 1978).

One major finding in the mind-body interaction is that anxiety, an emotional state, is highly dependent on muscle tension, a body state. A reduction in muscle tension results in a corresponding reduction in anxiety. The impact of fears and phobias can be relieved by relaxation and general arousal-reduction techniques. This principle is useful in assisting students who are experiencing severe test anxiety.

Most psychophysiological symptoms are treated through techniques that reduce general body and muscle arousal. Hypertension, fear of taking tests, physiological responses to stress, headaches, and a multitude of other body symptoms are relieved by the arousal-reduction techniques employed in formal therapeutic programs. The results of applying these skills to performance enhancement goals parallel the results obtained by persons who are generally highly competent. The implication is that body awareness and the control of autonomic functions are learnable skills that can be useful in the pursuit of academic excellence.

Biofeedback techniques have assisted many indivduals in learning muscle control. Body temperature control has also been taught effectively by biofeedback systems (Shapiro and Surwit, 1980). A long list of self-management techniques can be included in a curriculum on the self-management of body-sensory experience. Biofeedback training and progressive relaxation training are the two standard techniques, but they can be supplemented with meditation approaches (Carrington, 1977), imagery exercises (Lazarus, 1977), self-hypnosis (LeCron, 1970), and autogenic training (Luthe, 1963).

It is certainly not a novel idea to introduce sensory control techniques into the academic setting. Many high schools have offered courses in meditation, yoga, t'ai Chi Chuan, and other forms of body control exercises. The difference here is that application of these techniques to behavioral, interpersonal, and cognitive skills development maximizes their impact on academic performance goals.

Imagery Skills Training. Lazarus (1977) contends that we are unable to perform in reality what we cannot first imagine. The suggestion is that human performance is first blueprinted in the imaginal areas of the brain before it is actually performed. This hypothesis remains untested, but there is considerable evidence that developing one's imagery capacity significantly facilitates one's performance (Singer and Pope, 1978). Once again, the idea of teaching imagery techniques is not new, but integration of these techniques into a holistic personality management and enhancement program for underprepared college students has not yet been fully explored.

Emotional Skills Training. The affective modality presents special problems for self-control training. Many individuals who are effective in controlling their emotions do not know how they do it. There is no direct self-control intervention for balancing emotion. It is known that the cognitive, sensory, and interpersonal techniques already discussed here contribute to a balanced emotional state.

The most practical view of emotional control is drawn from the work of cognitive psychologists, such as Beck (1976) and Ellis (1977). Burns (1980) recently published a book that could serve as a curriculum outline for emotional management skills development. Building on Beck's work, Burns outlines ways of coping with intense negative emotions, such as guilt, depression, and feelings of worthlessness and hopelessness. In short, the negative feelings so detrimental to human performance, yet so common in daily experience, can be managed to reduce their negative impact.

Bloomfield and Kory (1980) address the other side of mood control, the cultivation of pleasure and joy. In their book *Inner Joy*, they describe a series of exercises and activities that support pleasure and satisfying emotion. They demonstrate how pleasurable events can energize productive activity. These two books together can exemplify the contents of the mood management component of a general program in self-management.

Health Enhancement Skills. To complete the full spectrum of personality modalities, the internal, or biological, biochemical aspects of personality must be included. These aspects reflect the individual's health habits. The relationship between diet and alertness and other performance attributes has long been recognized by physicians. Recently, the area of behavioral medicine (Davidson and Davidson, 1980) has organized information that is relevant to the health management component of the program recommended here.

The essential message of a behavioral medicine component is that life-style affects health. This connection can be systematically examined to demonstrate the level of personal control feasible in the management of personal health. Cormier and others (1980) devised a campus-based program directed at improving student health practices. This program includes five components: management of stress, increased physical activity, assertiveness, management of leisure and sleep, and management of eating patterns. Life-style, as defined by these writers, does not include all the personality domains, but it does represent a much broader definition than one typically encounters.

The Multimodal Approach to Personal Enhancement

Lazarus (1976, 1977, 1981) has pointed out that effective individual functioning is an interactive process between personality modalities. When applied to underprepared students (Nieves, 1978a) the multimodal approach seeks to help students to learn how to make adjustments in the ways that they behave, feel, sense, imagine, think, and relate to others. For each individual, a balance of these modalities supports optimum performance. In his search for the personality variables that champion athletes have in common, Mahoney (1979a) discovered that some athletes knew that they performed better under a high state of arousal. These athletes knew how to get aroused and maintain that arousal. Other athletes knew that they performed better in a low arousal state, and they learned how to relax and maintain calmness and coolness. The two key principles were, first, knowing the conditions under which they performed best and, second, knowing how to obtain and maintain those conditions.

Arousal or relaxation of the body is a controllable state that affects individuals differently. Knowing how to discover its impact on oneself is a personality skill that should be taught as part of a personal growth and development program in a learning center. Athletes learn how to obtain and maintain concentration or to focus attention. This is not a trait but a skill. Learning it and applying it is a necessary condition for athletic performance or any high-performance situation. It is also a key tool for effective academic performance.

The multimodal framework provides an easy self-assessment approach that helps students to pinpoint personality areas needing development in order for them to achieve their goals of academic performance. This method is well demonstrated in a manual specifically designed for minority students (Nieves, 1978a). The manual begins by teaching the multimodal assessment approach; then it teaches specific self-help interventions for a series of problems commonly associated with minority students in college. These include assertiveness training for dealing with interpersonal problems, reframing and cognitive restructuring techniques for mood problems, reading and study techniques for academic problems, and relaxation techniques for test and other anxiety management. The book also includes information units on career decision making and graduate education.

Self-Help Resource Materials

Coinciding with developments in cognitive and behavioral clinical and counseling areas, self-help materials have proliferated in recent years. These materials have been reviewed by Goetz and Etzel (1978) and Mahoney and Arnkoff (1980). While the literature in general and these reviews in particular fail to support unequivocally the superiority of self-control procedures over other interventions, they do support the general efficacy of these procedures. Self-control procedures and skills can be effective. Indeed, they can represent the most important outcome of any educational or psychological intervention program.

Davis, McKay, and Eshelman (1980) developed a workbook to help individuals to learn and apply stress-reduction techniques. They are extremely successful in their use of the bibliotherapeutic route to teach self-hypnosis, meditation, time management, progressive relaxation, and other effective stress-reduction techniques. This type of manual, in conjunction with a structured learning experience, can provide the basis for teaching self-control skills as they relate to the reduction of undue stress.

The U.S. Air Force human resources faculty has developed a study skills package (Dobrovolny, McCombs, and Judd, 1980). Evaluation of the package in its developmental stage shows that it is effective in increasing reading comprehension, memorization, and concentration. What is especially valuable about this manual is that it treats memorization, concentration, and comprehension as learnable skills, not as traits or immutable attributes. Consequently, the focus is on learning skills that help students to pursue their goals more effectively. Once learned, these skills can be applied to the full range of life areas.

Other materials are being developed almost daily. Valuable books that teach self-management principles include Rudenstam's (1980) primer on self-change and Watson and Tharp's (1972) classic book on self-modification procedures for personal adjustment. Williams and Long (1975) offer a very concise manual and test on developing a self-managed life-style. Mahoney (1979b) focuses his manual on strategies for solving personal problems. Thus, the material for a comprehensive curriculum on teaching self-management skills is already available, researched, and reviewed. Although a great deal more needs to be done, there is sufficient evidence to support full application in a well-defined academic support program.

The literature reports extensive applications of self-management principles to both educational and psychological domains. It has been applied with elementary school children in a classroom setting (Workman and Hector, 1978) and to the academic problems of special populations (Beneke and Harris, 1972; Ziesat, Rosenthal, and White, 1978). Clinical applications have included insomnia (Mitchell and White, 1977), depression or mood control (Deutsch, 1978), anxiety management (Deffenbacher and Micheals, 1980), assertiveness problems (Craighead, 1979), psychosomatic and pain control problems (Leigh, 1978), substance abuse (Blittner and Goldberg, 1978), impulsivity control (Hanna, 1978), and weight control (Cohen and others, 1980).

The application of self-management materials is generally conducted in a narrow, unimodal framework. However, human performance is extremely complex, and it is expressed through the full range of personality modalities. Academic and college adjustment problems are complex and not amenable to single-method approaches. Consequently, any effort of intervention or education aimed at a single problem usually fails to produce a thorough and comprehensive impact on all the personality domains. The multimodal framework contends that change, like the problem itself, is an interrelated, interconnected personality experience. Consequently, change and enhancement efforts must be directed at the entire personality, not just at one or two domains. Likewise, self-management strategies directed at a single domain, say impulse control, fail to offer self-management strategies for accompanying thoughts or interpersonal skills associated with impulse control.

Because the learning and adjustment problems of the underprepared students in the nation's colleges are broad and include both educational and psychological domains, a self-management program must also be comprehensive and integrated. It must include behavioral self-management skills as well as affective, sensory, imagery, cognitive, interpersonal, and physical health self-management skills.

Motivation: First, Key, and Final Ingredient

Motivation to change or learn is an important question in the consideration of self-management issues. Like most educational and psychological intervention strategies, self-management approaches rely on the individual's motivation. Essentially, persons seek the best possible conditions for survival and development. Unless there is exceptionally strong evidence to the contrary, educators must approach their students on the assumption that students want to succeed.

In the numerous workshops, lectures, and courses on self-managment applications that have been held in recent years, the question most often raised by audiences involves the so-called unmotivated student. Usually, the question refers to the experience that many have had of working with students who do not cooperate with the intervention strategy proposed. These students are frequently referred to as *resistant*.

The view that supports the use of self-management interventions is that resistance—or, rather, lack of cooperation—suggests that these students do not agree with the formulation accorded the problem. As a result, they will not cooperate with the educator's efforts to resolve the problem. For any intervention to succeed, students must believe and cooperate with the intervention strategy, both privately and publicly. Thus, it is not enough for them to cooperate in behavior. They must also think and feel in concurrence with both the formulation of the problem and the approach prescribed for its resolution. Although this in itself is not sufficient to ensure success, it is a necessary condition for any successful educational or psychological intervention. The point that I am making here is that motivation for treatment, whether for problem resolution or just for personal enhancement, is an integral part of the functioning human being. The most logical step for the practitioner who encounters opposition to an educational or psychological intervention is to examine the student's description of the problem or problems and the proposed resolution in search of grounds for concurrence between student and educator.

Self-management assumptions do not differ from the assumptions that support all educational efforts. Teaching self-management techniques builds on the natural motivation of individuals to better their own condition. It is the definition of the condition and the betterment that becomes the focal point. Students usually act in a way that is consistent

88

with their definition of what is better. With motivation and goal thereby established, the question then becomes one of how? Self-management strategies provide an exceptionally good answer to that question, because they leave the student ultimately in control. To increase motivation or willingness to cooperate, information must be provided that will increase students' conviction that the problems can be resolved and that the means to resolving them lie within their own ability and control.

Conclusions

Educators and others who work with adult populations in the nation's adult education classes, in psychological consulting rooms, and in medical offices frequently hear their clients ask, "Why didn't they teach me that in school?" This question reflects the realization by many adults that, if the information just acquired had been utilized at an earlier point in their lives, they would have avoided certain mistakes.

The learning centers in American colleges are dealing with students who are already learning useful things much later in their lives than others do. This situation is aggravated if the learning center students are not taught how to teach themselves. Self-management skills are self-teaching skills. The skill to learn from and by oneself is ultimately the most useful and effective tool in education.

When a learning center offers students self-management skills, it is not like giving a fish to a hungry man but rather like teaching the man to fish for himself. This assertion reflects the essential message of this chapter: By utilizing a multimodal framework, self-help strategies can be effectively integrated into the learning center program.

Many questions remain to be answered. For example, the material contained in the self-management curriculum can be taught in the context of counseling, classroom, and group sessions, or some combination thereof. Yet there has been no careful investigation to date of which method works best for which population. Like much of the other material taught in a learning center, a self-management skills curriculum can best be evaluated by offering the course and evaluating the results.

References

Bandura, A. "Self-Efficacy: Toward a Unifying Theory of Behavioral Change." *Psychological Review*, 1977, *84*, 191–215.
Beck, A. T. *Cognitive Therapy and the Emotional Disorders*. New York: International University Press, 1976.
Beneke, W. M., and Harris, M. B. "Teaching Self-Control of Study Behavior." *Behavior Research and Therapy*, 1972, *10* (5), 669–675.

89

Blittner, M., and Goldberg, J. "Cognitive Self-Control Factors in the Reduction of Smoking Behavior." *Behavior Therapy*, 1978, *9* (4), 553–561.

Bloomfield, H. H., and Kory, R. B. *Inner Joy: New Strategies for Adding More Pleasure to Your Life.* New York: Wyden Books, 1980.

Burns, D. D. *Feeling Good: The New Mood Therapy.* New York: Morrow, 1980.

Carrington, P. *Freedom in Meditation.* New York: Doubleday, 1977.

Cohen, E. A., Gelfand, D. M., Dodd, D. K., Jensen, J., and Turner, C. "Weight Loss Maintenance in Children and Adolescents." *Behavior Therapy*, 1980, *11* (1), 26–37.

Cormier, A., Prefontaine, M., MacDonald, H., and Stuart, R. "Life-style Change on the Campus: A Pilot Test of a Program to Improve Student Health Practices." In P. O. Davidson and S. M. Davidson (Eds.), *Behavioral Medicine: Changing Health Lifestyles.* New York: Brunner/Mazel, 1980.

Craighead, L. W. "Self-Instructional Training for Assertive-Refusal Behavior." *Behavior Therapy*, 1979, *10* (4), 529–542.

Davidson, P. O., and Davidson, S. M. (Eds.). *Behavioral Medicine: Changing Health Life styles.* New York: Brunner/Mazel, 1980.

Davis, M., McKay, M., and Eshelman, E. R. *The Relaxation and Stress Reduction Workbook.* Richmond, Calif.: Harbinger, 1980.

Deffenbacher, J. L., and Micheals, A. C. "Two Self-Control Procedures in the Reduction of Targeted and Nontargeted Anxieties: A Year Later." *Journal of Counseling Psychology*, 1980, *27* (1), 9–15.

Deutsch, A. "Self-Control and Depression: An Appraisal." *Behavior Therapy*, 1978, *9* (3), 410–414.

Dobrovolny, J. L., McCombs, B. L., and Judd, W. A. *Study Skills Package: Development and Evaluation.* Lowery Air Force Base, Colo.: Air Force Human Resources Laboratory Technical Training Division, 1980.

Ellis, A. "The Basic Clinical Theory of Rational-Emotive Therapy." In A. Ellis and R. Grieger (Eds.), *Handbook of Rational-Emotive Therapy.* New York: Springer, 1977.

Garner, A. "A Comprehensive College Model for Learning Assistance Centers." In K. V. Lauridsen (Ed.), *New Directions for College Learning Assistance: Examining the Scope of Learning Centers,* no. 1. San Francisco: Jossey-Bass, 1980.

Goetz, E. M., and Etzel, B. C. "A Brief Review of Self-Control Procedures: Problems and Solutions." *The Behavioral Therapist*, 1978, *1* (5), 5–8.

Gottman, J., Notarius, C., Gonso, J., and Harkman, H. *A Couples Guide to Communication.* Champaign, Ill.: Research Press, 1976.

Hanna, R. "Self-Control: Monitoring the Target Behavior Versus Monitoring a Competing Response." *Journal of Counseling Psychology*, 1978, *25* (5), 473–475.

Lange, A. J., and Jakubowski, P. *Responsible Assertive Behavior.* Champaign, Ill.: Research Press, 1976.

Lazarus, A. A. "New Methods in Psychotherapy: A Case Study." *South African Medical Journal*, 1958, *32*, 660–664.

Lazarus, A. A. "Multimodal Behavior Therapy: Treatment of the Basic Id." *Journal of Nervous and Mental Disease*, 1973, *156*, 404–411.

Lazarus, A. A. "Multimodal Assessment." In A. A. Lazarus (Ed.), *Multimodal Behavioral Therapy.* New York: Springer, 1976.

Lazarus, A. A. *In the Mind's Eye: The Power of Imagery Therapy to Give You Control over Your Life.* New York: Rowsen Associates, 1977.

Lazarus, A. A. "Multimodal Behavior Therapy." Part III. In E. Shostrom (Ed.), *Three Approaches to Psychotherapy II.* (Three sixteen millimeter films or three-quarter inch video casettes). Orange, Calif.: Psychological Films, 1978.

Lazarus, A. A. *The Practice of Multimodal Therapy Toward the Art and Science of Effective Psychotherapy.* New York: McGraw-Hill, 1981.

Lazarus, A. A., and Fay, A. *I Can If I Want To.* New York: Morrow, 1975.

Lazarus, A. A., and Nieves, L. R. "Assertiveness Training in the Multimodal Therapy Framework." *Comprehensive Psychotherapy,* 1980, *1*, 39–46.

LeCron, L. *Self-Hypnosis.* New York: New American Library, 1970.

Leigh, H. "Self-Control, Biofeedback, and Change in Psychosomatic Approaches." *Psychotherapy and Psychosomatics,* 1978, *30* (3–4), 198–204.

Luthe, W. "Autogenic Training: Method, Research, and Applications in Medicine." *American Journal of Psychotherapy,* 1963, *17*, 174–195.

Mahoney, M. J. "Cognitive Skills and Athletic Performance." In P. C. Kendall and S. D. Holhen (Eds.), *Cognitive-Behavioral Interventions: Theory, Research, and Procedures.* New York: Academic Press, 1979a.

Mahoney, M. J. *Self-Change: Strategies for Solving Personal Problems.* New York: Norton, 1979b.

Mahoney, M. J., and Arnkoff, D. B. "Self-Management." In O. F. Pomerleau and J. P. Brady (Eds.), *Behavioral Medicine: Theory and Practice.* Baltimore: Williams and Wilkins, 1980.

Meichenbaum, D. "A Self-Instructional Approach to Stress Management: A Proposal for Stress Inoculation Training." In S. Sarason and C. O. Speilberger (Eds.), *Stress and Anxiety.* Vol. 2. New York: Wiley, 1975.

Mitchell, K. R., and White, R. G. "Self-Management of Severe Predormital Insomnia." *Journal of Behavior Therapy and Experimental Psychiatry,* 1977, *8* (1), 57–63.

Nieves, L. R. *College Achievement Through Self-Help: A Planning and Guidance Manual for Minority Students.* Princeton, N.J.: Educational Testing Service, 1978a.

Nieves, L. R. *The Minority College Student Experience: A Case for the Use of Self-Control Systems.* Princeton, N.J.: Educational Testing Service, 1978b.

Rudenstam, K. E. *Methods of Self-Change: An ABC Primer.* Monterey, Calif.: Brooks/Cole, 1980.

Salter, A. *Conditional Reflex Therapy.* New York: Farrar, Straus, 1949.

Shapiro, D., and Surwit, R. S. "Biofeedback." In O. F. Pomerleau and J. P. Brady (Eds.), *Behavioral Medicine: Theory and Practice.* Baltimore: Williams and Wilkins, 1980.

Singer, J. L., and Pope, K. S. (Eds.). *The Power of Human Imagination: New Methods in Psychotherapy.* New York: Plenum Press, 1978.

Sullivan, L. L. "Growth and Influence of the Learning Center Movement." In K. V. Lauridsen (Ed.), *New Directions for College Learning Assistance: Examining the Scope of Learning Centers,* no. 1. San Francisco: Jossey-Bass, 1980.

Watson, D. L., and Tharp, R. G. *Self-Directed Behavior: Self-Modification for Personal Adjustment.* Monterey, Calif.: Brooks/Cole, 1972.

Whyte, C. B. "An Integrated Counseling and Learning Center for a Liberal Arts College." In K. V. Lauridsen (Ed.), *New Directions for College Learning Assistance: Examining the Scope of Learning Centers,* no. 1. San Francisco: Jossey-Bass, 1980.

Williams, R. L., and Long, J. D. *Toward a Self-Managed Life Style.* Boston: Houghton Mifflin, 1975.

Woolfolk, R. L., and Richardson, F. C. *Stress, Sanity, and Survival.* New York: Monarch Press, 1978.

Workman, E. A., and Hector, M. A. "Behavioral Self-Control in Classroom Settings: A Review of the Literature." *Journal of School Psychology*, 1978, *16* (3), 227-236.

Ziesat, H. A., Rosenthal, T. L., and White, G. M. "Behavioral Self-Control in Treating Procrastination of Studying." *Psychological Reports*, 1978, *42* (1), 59-69.

Luis Nieves is associate director of the Office for Minority Education at Educational Testing Service, Princeton, New Jersey. Former dean of student affairs at Livingston College of Rutgers University, he has published extensively in the fields of psychology and minority education.

The editor summarizes the volume and discusses
learning centers and special student groups.

Learning Centers and Special Student Groups: The 1980s

Lester Wilson

Common Themes

Three themes have emerged as the authors of these chapters have developed their ideas on learning centers and special student groups. Each theme is inclusive in nature and applicable to other student groups and different college or university environments. The overriding concern, at least in terms of the questions raised in this volume, is that special student groups should be helped to enter the mainstream of their academic communities as quickly and efficaciously as possible. A second concern is that centers should be comprehensive and have service delivery systems that can be of use to the entire student population. Finally, the authors agree that individualized attention is important to the particular student groups being considered and that the learning center is the campus organization most capable of providing this kind of service.

Mainstreaming. The ultimate goal of all supportive academic and counseling services and programs is to facilitate access to the college or university mainstream. The length of time it will take students from one of the special groups discussed in this volume to achieve this end will

L. Wilson (Ed.). *New Directions for College Learning Assistance:*
Helping Special Student Groups, no. 7. San Francisco: Jossey-Bass, March 1982.

depend not only on the quality and comprehensiveness of supportive services available to them, but on other variables as well—on their skills proficiency levels, on their determination to persevere, on pressures and responsibilities related to the family or to a work situation, and on the academic standards of their chosen college or university. The reader will have noted in the articles by Rosenthal and Hirtz that this goal of mainstreaming special groups underlies all their discussions of techniques and strategies for assisting students with physical and/or learning disabilities. Similarly, Collins and Wilson are equally concerned with assisting underprepared students associated with their programs to branch out and become fully participatory in campus academic life. At Cornell, for instance, COSEP students are expected to become fully independent learners by the end of their sophomore year; at LIU/Brooklyn the same philosophy prevails, although this process can be more prolonged. Nieves, while discussing the issue from a more general perspective, argues that self-management techniques can be taught to all student groups and that these processes are necessary for a student to be reasonably competitive as a college or university undergraduate.

The role of learning centers in helping students attain this status should not be underestimated nor should it be oversold. It is true that learning centers are admirably suited to delivering academic and counseling services that would be difficult, if not impossible, to find elsewhere on campus. It is also important, however, for learning center staff members to assess realistically the limitations inherent in learning center services so that they do not view themselves as replacements or substitutes for the traditional university instructional staff or as completely revolutionizing customary pedagogical procedures—lectures, classroom assignments, examinations. In the final analysis, the main purpose of these centers (as far as the students discussed in this volume are concerned) is to help these students adjust and adapt to the rigorous demands of the academic world. It should be extremely rewarding for those who are associated with these centers to know that their help will directly affect the chances these students will have for access to the mainstream and for an eventual successful conclusion of a college career.

Individualized Services. The major drawing card of the learning center in this mainstreaming process is that its staff members can give individualized attention to the diverse learning problems of students. Colleges and universities, for the most part, have few other facilities on campus for working with students in this way. Some particularly comprehensive programs, notably the Learning Center at Miami-Dade Community College, South Campus, have complex computerized instructional systems in which students are carefully tracked, counseled, programmed, tested, and taught on an individual basis. Although this sophisticated and very expensive operation is probably well beyond the reach of most learning centers, the prospect of being able to work individually and efficiently with large numbers of students is very attractive.

For the student groups discussed in this sourcebook, individualization of services is of paramount importance. Klosek provides many illustrations of ways in which learning centers can serve ESL students individually. A major consideration, he argues, is that "one should teach what is appropriate to the proficiency level of the student." It is true that ESL students can be readily grouped according to language competencies, but the learning center can go one step beyond this traditional approach, and, through laboratories and tutoring, work with each student individually. Again, this kind of attention will be difficult to find elsewhere on campus.

Comprehensive Service Delivery Systems. One argument that has surfaced repeatedly in this *New Directions for College Learning Assistance* series is that the learning center of the 1980s should be conceptualized in terms of its breadth of services and the diversity of student groups it intends to assist. In this same vein, Collins and Wilson find program or learning center exclusiveness counterproductive and urge that they attempt an expansion in their service delivery system to accommodate all students. The isolated center, reserved for one or two special student groups, will only discourage the students they are supposed to help. Not only will they feel that some sort of stigma is attached to using a learning center if they see themselves as the only group receiving assistance, but the rest of the university community will also tend to regard these centers as places reserved for special, designated, "peripheral" groups. Coleman develops this concept from an historical perspective and points out that many learning centers were originally outgrowths of opportunity program supportive services components. As such, they were legally restricted to serving a single student group. However, the proliferation of these centers has meant that an accommodation has been necessary to allow for keeping the original mandate intact while at the same time expanding center services in order to assist the general student population.

Maintaining a Spirit of Innovation

Most learning centers were born in the 1970s in an atmosphere of intense dedication and commitment on the part of their academic and counseling staff members. In spite of the difficulties so many students seemed to be having with the demands of college life, these centers have remained outposts of optimism and innovation. Today, after years of experience in the field and at a time when fiscal stringencies will weigh heavily on the entire academic community, learning center personnel will no doubt find it less easy to sustain the enthusiasm they once felt so strongly. The need for innovative approaches to learning, however, will be just as great in the 1980s as it was in the early days of learning center development. Staff members, therefore, must still be prepared to come up with new ideas and to devise additional supportive services that can be incorporated into the daily operations of their centers. Only in so doing will they truly serve the needs of their students; they will also find this process self-regenerative in that infusions of new concepts and methodologies will help to make their day-to-day routines more personally rewarding and intellectually stimulating.

In light of the presentations that the authors of these chapters have made concerning learning center services for their particular student groups, the reader may find it helpful to consider a few possibilities for innovation that may be explored in the years to come. These ideas are only a sampling of the wide spectrum of services that can be incorporated into the learning center structure. Their implementation, however, will mean that all student groups will be better served; learning center personnel, also, will find that these new approaches can be useful in sustaining their enthusiasm for their work.

Student Acclimization. Students who fit one or more of the categories discussed in this issue are likely to have little or no background in the realities of academic life. Underprepared students, for example, are usually first-generation collegians and are easily intimidated by their first encounter with this new and frequently threatening experience. Students with physical or learning disabilities, likewise, will feel strange and somewhat alien in the rushed, frenetic atmosphere of the first freshman weeks on campus. The ESL students will have similar anxieties. Not only will they be obliged to adapt to a new country with its different customs and practices, but they will also find the American college or university far different from institutions at a comparable level in their country of origin. Unfortunately, underprepared ESL students will face an additional stressful situation, one that comes along with their poor academic skills.

Some campuses have elaborate orientation programs for entering freshmen, replete with information booklets, formal workshops, and informal social functions. Others leave students to fend for themselves as best they can. In both cases, they probably leave out important pieces of information that would make a student's adjustment to campus life a much more agreeable process. Learning centers can convey this information, either through study-skills workshops or by way of a developmental reading program. The topics that are suggested in the paragraphs below are by no means exhaustive and are meant to be viewed as a starter.

College Jargon. Academic terminology that learning center staff members take for granted will seem like a foreign language to many of the students discussed in this volume. *Bursar, dean, faculty, curriculum, liberal arts, humanities*—such terms will probably seem strange, and, if students do not understand their meanings, they will likely feel even more anxious in an already stressful situation. Learning center staff members can prepare glossaries of these terms that can be given to all incoming freshmen.

Helpful Tips. How many students know how to approach their instructors? What are some ways of asking questions tactfully so that they do not seem hostile, rude, or unduly insistent? How are students supposed to use the library and its resources? Where are the best places on campus for periods of quiet study? These are not idle questions, although they probably will not be answered in a traditional freshman orientation program. Sometime, very early in a student's stay on campus, answers should be forthcoming. Learning centers can assign peer tutors who already have had a few semesters on campus to give advice to the neophytes. This can be done on an individual basis, or in a larger workshop format.

Career Information. Several authors in this volume have touched on the topic of career guidance as it relates to their special student groups. Learning centers usually are not equipped to offer this kind of counseling, but staff members will need to know where on campus their students may seek advice about career possibilities. In cases where career counseling services for disabled students are minimal, listings of off-campus counseling services should be available to these students and to learning center personnel as well. Outside professionals should also be invited to offer workshops and participate in informal sessions with disabled students who are concerned about career possibilities. As an adjunct to these career information activities, the learning center staff should be able to direct students to part-time job opportunities, particularly in the case of the ESL student who will be restricted to working on campus.

Participation in Campus Activities. There is perhaps no more effective way of completing the process of mainstreaming students from the special groups discussed in this volume than by having them join clubs and otherwise participate in campus-wide activities. They will get a much better picture of their relationship to the campus as a whole and will be less prone to feelings of intimidation when in the classroom. Encouragement for this sort of activity is not something learning centers can easily institutionalize, but it deserves to be done on an informal basis. Frequently, a student will not feel a part of the academic and social activities around him until he gets out, by himself, joins a club or takes up with a social or political interest group.

Community Outreach. As learning centers move away from exclusiveness and expand their services to suit the needs of a more diverse student populaton, they can also begin to explore the possibilities of using their expertise to assist individuals and groups outside the university community. Outreach can be done in a variety of ways and should be projected only on the basis of local needs. The two examples that follow should be seen in this light and are presented here only for purposes of illustration. Both were outgrowths of learning center activities at the Brooklyn Center of Long Island University.

Children's Institute. Collins and Wilson mention in their chapter that the tutorial services component was at the core of learning center services at LIU/Brooklyn. Over the years, some of the university students who were being tutored would bring their children in for help. Also, parents of elementary school children began to make inquiries and students from the local high school would come to see if tutors were available to them. In time, the original core of undergraduate and graduate tutors was augmented by professional reading and mathematics specialists and organized into a small Children's Institute. Wednesday evening and Saturday morning small-group classes are currently scheduled in the basic skills areas, but instruction is also given to gifted children as well. The children are pretested to determine areas of weakness and strength and required to bring recommendations from their classroom teachers for their activities in the Children's Institute. The ten-week semester is followed by posttesting, after which the parents are given a formal report on each child's progress. This report is particularly important in cases where a teacher has required supplemental work as a condition for promotion to the next grade. In its direct benefit to the LIU/Brooklyn Learning Center, the Children's Institute permits learning center personnel, most of whom are part-time employees, to earn additional money and this also increases their willingness to remain at the Center on a less than full-time basis. Finally, since tuition is charged for the ten-week session, the Learning Center has been able to generate outside revenue and show that some operational costs can be underwritten independently of university support.

Community Service. The LIU/Brooklyn Learning Center has worked in conjunction with the Brooklyn Educational and Cultural Alliance (BECA), a consortium of private universities and cultural institutions, to provide basic skills instruction and academic and career counseling to various community groups in Brooklyn. BECA, which is funded by the New York State Department of Education, solicits proposals from Brooklyn-based community groups for academic and cultural services that are then provided by the member institutions. If the proposals are approved, the community groups are awarded sufficient funds for implementation. Some groups have asked for learning center-related services, and staff members have gone out into various communities to set up tutorial programs or offer courses in the basic skills. Again, this kind of outreach has not only been beneficial to the community groups served, but it has also meant that the Learning Center has been able to retain competent personnel who might have gone elsewhere in search of more highly-paid positions.

The Computer. As this decade progresses, learning center personnel should be acutely aware of the usefulness of computers and they should be prepared to incorporate them into their daily operational routines. Computers have become so much a part of American life that they are available and affordable for home use. Alfred Bork at a 1979 Convention of the Association for the Development of Computer-Based Instructional Systems outlined some of the positive contributions computers could be expected to make to higher education: "The first change to be noted in the universities is that computers will allow more effective learning situations. The computer will be very competitive with many of the modes of learning, such as the lecture situation, now common in universities. Even the textbook may be threatened as the increasing cost of books is now putting them in a category where electronic delivery of the same material, through both school and home machines, will soon be cheaper than paper delivery." Colleges and universities, Bork argued, cannot ignore the potential of these machines, particularly since they are almost the only items associated with education whose costs are decreasing.

Computer Assisted Instruction (CAI) has been hailed as the new campus miracle; it has also been derided as just another American mechanical toy and fad. A reasoned evaluation of CAI effectiveness obviously falls somewhere in between, but its potential for providing complementary support services to students in a learning enter setting is so great that directors and staff members must make a point of thoroughly investigating this field. Learning centers must be able to tap this new educational tool and make realistic and constructive use of it. This is not to suggest that human services will in any way become superfluous. Hirtz, in discussing the special needs of physically disabled students, makes it quite clear that human assistance will always be needed by his student group. He also argues that there are some things that machines can do better. In the final analysis, the learning center cannot afford to ignore the merits of CAI; if it does, it will only reduce its future ability to effect innovative techniques and methodologies, which just as surely will be taken up and used effectively elsewhere on campus.

The 1980s

Forecasting the prospects for special student groups in higher education during the 1980s would be a foolhardy enterprise as this volume goes to press. In their chapter, Collins and Wilson suggest that this present decade will be one in which Americans are asked to make a choice either "to continue the liberal traditions of the previous two decades or reduce the funding on which so many students and academic support programs have depended." Although the full impact of the latest federal policies concerning higher education has not yet been felt, there is every reason to expect that colleges and universities—administrators, faculty, and students alike—will be adversely affected by the budget decisions that are currently being made in Washington. Some learning centers will find their operating budget lines reduced; others will be required to remain at current levels of funding. Learning center directors will need to solicit the support of campus deans and other high university officials actively if they are to preserve the integrity and effectiveness of their centers.

There is at least one certainty, however, in this general atmosphere of flux and dislocation. For the moment, it is highly unlikely that colleges and universities will see any marked improvement in the academic skills levels of their incoming freshman classes. Indeed, articles in magazines and newspapers have regularly attempted to expose the lack of adequate preparation that young people now receive in the nation's secondary schools. They predict that this situation will almost certainly deteriorate further in the 1980s. Consequently, the number of underprepared students will increase and colleges and universities will still be called on to provide the necessary support services to bring these students up to acceptable levels of academic proficiency. Where does the learning center fit in this picture? In answer to this question, it is difficult to imagine that this service will not find a place on the college campus, particularly in view of its often-demonstrated role in upgrading students' academic skills levels.

The task of bringing students into the mainstream of college life can be Herculean; it can also be a very rewarding human experience. Learning center personnel, very much in the midst of this struggle, can see at first hand some of the changes in students who are part of the special groups discussed in this sourcebook. They have been called upon to devise a host of new educational techniques and strategies in order to respond to the needs of their students. Although they have not always been successful, the basic philosophical principle has never been altered or put aside. Students who do not have the background for college-level work can catch up. Learning centers contribute substantially to this process, although they do so cooperatively with other campus departments and organizations. Ultimately, colleges and universities have made an enormous differences in the lives of thousands of students making it possible for them to attain their professonal goals and to enter the intellectual and economic mainstream of American society at a completely different level of participation.

Reference

Bork, A. "Computers and Educational Institutions." Paper published in the *Proceedings of the Annual Convention of the Association for the Development of Computer-Based Instructional Systems,* vol. 3, San Diego, February 27–March 1, 1979.

Lester Wilson is director of Special Academic Services at the Brooklyn Center of Long Island University.

Index

A

Academic Therapy Publications, 62
Access: excellence reconciled with, 3–17; factors in, 20
Affective factors, assessment of, 4–5
Alexander, L. G., 70, 73
American Chemical Society, 42
American Council on Education, 60, 62
Anxiety: and self-management training, 82, 85; in underprepared students, 27–28
Arnkoff, D. B., 85, 90
Arousal, self-management of, 84–85
Assertiveness training, 81–82
Assessment: of freshmen, 4–6, in mathematics, 6
Association for Children with Learning Disabilities, 61
Association for the Development of Computer-Based Instructional Systems, 99
Association of Learning-Disabled Adults, 62
Astin, A., 11, 16

B

Bandura, A., 77, 88
Baudoin, E. M., 69, 74
Beck, A. T., 80, 83, 88
Behavioral skills, self-management training for, 79–80
Beneke, W. M., 86, 88
Bingham, G., 61
Blittner, M., 86, 89
Bloom, B., 4, 16
Bloomfield, H. H., 83–84, 89
Bok, D., 7, 16
Bork, A., 99, 101
Boyan, D. R., 65, 74
Boykin A. W., 31
Brooklyn Center. See Long Island University
Brooklyn College-City University of

New York, developmental courses at, 10
Brooks, I., 9, 16
Brown, D., 60
Brown, D. R., 31
Bruffee, K., 8, 16
Burns, D. D., 83, 89
Byrd, D., 68, 70, 74

C

California, Berkeley, University of, Professional Development Program at, 6
California, Los Angeles, University of, re-education at, 8
California Achievement Test, 67
Caputo-Ferrara, E., 59–63
Carnegie Council on Policy Studies in Higher Education, 6, 16
Carrington, P., 83, 89
Centra, J. A., 30
Chambers, M. M., 30
Christ, F., 61
City University of New York: Brooklyn College of, 10; and open admissions, 24
Closer Look: National Information Center for the Handicapped, 62
Cognitive skills, self-management training in, 80–81
Cohen, E. A., 86, 89
Coleman, J. E., 2, 3–17, 95
College Entrance Examination Board, 60
Collins, W., 19–32, 94, 95, 98, 100
Communications skills, for underprepared students, 82
Competence. See Self-management skills
Computer-assisted instruction, and learning centers, 99
Corder, S. P., 72, 74
Cormier, A., 84, 89
Cornelius, E. T., 70, 73
Cornell University, Committee on